a pocket guide to

cacti and
succulents

a pocket guide to

cacti and succulents

Terry Hewitt

GREENWICH
EDITIONS

Photo Credits:

All photographs featured in this book are part of the Chrysalis Image Library. Digital images © Chrysalis Image Library/Simon Clay, taken at Hollygate Cactus Nursery, Sussex, England.

This edition published in 2004 by
Greenwich Editions
The Chrysalis Building
Bramley Road, London W10 6SP

An imprint of **Chrysalis** Books Group

Produced by
PRC Publishing Limited
The Chrysalis Building
Bramley Road, London W10 6SP

An imprint of **Chrysalis** Books Group

ISBN 0 86288 696 1

Printed and bound in Malaysia

Contents

Introduction

"Bizarre," "gaunt," "weird," "compact," "symmetrical," "sculptural," "architectural," "exotic," are just a few of the words often used by people to describe these plants. Many liken them to other objects such as starfish, silver dollars, sea urchins, stones, candles, sticks, and many more too numerous to mention.

Cacti and succulent plants have developed over the centuries to be able to survive under conditions that are hostile to most other plants. They are slow growing and would be easily swamped by lush vegetation.

Many are found in desert conditions (a desert means less than 10 inches (25cm) rainfall per year). Often these areas are rocky and hilly rather than Sahara-like and have a poor well-drained and often rocky soil. When there is rainfall it is usually seasonal, intermittent and infrequent. To supplement the rain, many plants have adapted shapes that provide good condensation points for the often-occurring night mists and fogs. Most species are quite specific in their natural requirements and although they may only occur in a small area, are often to be found on outcrops of similar natural formations within that area.

These fascinating plants are quite undemanding and adapted to survival under adverse conditions. This makes them ideal for the keen collector who can maintain certain basic standards. They are mostly not tolerant of prolonged low temperatures, boggy conditions, or low light levels. Light, temperature, and moisture are all interrelated so that an increase in one will require an increase in the others. Most people are able to grow the majority of species indoors on a sunny window sill, as cacti are tolerant of the lack of humidity in most modern

Totem pole cactus.

houses. They are also forgiving of any long periods of absence of their caretaker, as they are drought resistant.

There is, however, a considerable difference between survival and growing well and I hope that with a little more knowledge collectors will be able to achieve this. As readers will come from a wide range of temperature zones a certain amount of experimentation will be required to get the best under your own conditions. The cold, bleak, short winter days of the North bear no comparison to the longer, bright, frost-free areas nearer the Equator. Plants that need full sun in northern Europe or the northern U.S.A. may need shading when grown in Texas or Arizona.

The most important thing about growing plants is to enjoy them. It makes little difference to the plants, whether you call them Fred or Fiona; the only real use of a name is to be able to talk to somebody else about them, so that they understand you. The most important thing is to have fun with this great rewarding hobby.

PLANT GROUPS

Cacti and other succulent plants are usually linked together in the same group as both come from roughly the same latitudes and are adapted to surviving periods of drought. Although succulent plants can come from anywhere in the world, most of those cultivated grow between altitudes of 40N and 40S.

A succulent plant is one that stores moisture to carry it over periods of drought, unlike a xerophyte, which often has a more woody structure, or a bulb with an underground storage organ. Compared with xerophytes and bulbs, succulent plants are interesting for most of the year, even when dormant.

A succulent plant can store moisture in one of three ways: by having swollen leathery leaves; a thick swollen stem; or an underground (or partially so) storage organ. A cactus, on the other hand, is a member of the plant family Cactaceae. For a plant to be classified as a cactus, it must have certain botanical characteristics. It must be a perennial dicotyledon with a single-celled berry. The last characteristic is only found in the Cactaceae and it is called an areole. This is a modified auxiliary bud and it is from this little pad that spines, shoots, and flowers appear. Although areoles are clearly visible on many cacti such as the prickly pear, they are far less noticeable in the Christmas (winter-flowering) cactus, secreted in the notches of its flattened stems. So, it is true to say that all cacti are succulent, but not all succulents are cacti.

Cacti are natives of the New World, and grow just into Canada and south through the islands and mainland to Chile and Argentina. The only other "natural" occurrence of cacti is in Madagascar, where some epiphytic cacti with very sticky seeds grow on a migratory bird route. Many Old World succulents occur in much the same latitudes as those in the Americas and evolution has led to many similarly shaped plants developing. The largest group of cactus-like succulents is probably the *Euphorbia*, but a close inspection will show that they lack the areole.

Cacti

These can be split into two main groups; desert and rainforest plants.

Rainforest cacti are usually called epiphytic cacti, as they grow on other plants, which they clamber over. They feed on the pockets of humus that collect in various nooks and crannies. As moisture is not normally a problem in a rainforest, many of these plants have evolved long strap-like or slender pencil stems so that they can collect the maximum available light. The *Epiphyllum* and *Rhipsalis* are good examples of this type of cactus. In cultivation they require a bright position but protection from full sun and they grow better in warmer, damper, and more humid conditions.

The major and most cultivated group is the desert type. Although a very few have large tuberous roots and slender pencil-like stems, most have either globular or columnar stems. These plants have evolved over the centuries into strange but

Cactus being grown on ready for sale.

functional forms. Most have ribs or tubercles that support areoles and spines. The bodies are concertinaed so that they can expand rapidly when water is available and contract slowly when it is not, without splitting their skins. Most plants tend to point their crowns toward the sun, as these and their ribs cast cool shadows over the rest of the plant. The often dense spination and close ribs help to hold a micro-climate around the plant, again to cut down water loss. Most have thick waxy skins

Holly Gate Cactus Nursery, West Sussex, England.

with few pores to lower transpiration and further reduce water loss.

Seeds of the tall column cactus in the wild usually germinate in the shelter of other vegetation or rocks. After they have been established for several years, they will grow through their hosts to become the splendid sculptural specimens often seen in cactus country. Many of these are night-flowering, and open their buds at dusk, closing them in the morning as the heat of the sun rises. Plants lose a great deal of moisture through their flowers and this helps to conserve moisture. The flowers of the large-growing column cactus can be roughly divided into two groups. One group has large showy and often scented flowers and are usually pollinated by moths. The other group have smaller more chunky flowers with thicker leathery petals and sometimes a less than pleasant smell; these are usually pollinated by bats. There are also a number of smaller column cacti that have tubular flowers; these are designed to hold nectar to encourage the humming birds to visit them and pollinate them.

The cacti usually referred to as "globular" are initially this shape but with great age usually become shortly cylindrical, sometimes erect, sometimes creeping along the ground. Some are quite large like the barrel cactus but the majority have small individual heads although some of these will make large clumps with great age. A few of the rarer, slow-growing species have large swollen roots and grow almost flush with the ground, only the top being visible. Flowering takes place at different times of year and in areas where there are several species from the same genera, then these will usually flower at different times to avoid cross pollination and the risk of hybrids. The spring is probably the prime time for flowers.

Most cacti prefer a warm climate but a few come from areas that experience sub-zero temperatures in winter. The latter mostly come from very dry areas and are covered in snow in winter, which protects them to some degree. Most of these plants are difficult to grow in cultivation, as it is almost impossible to recreate their natural environment, with its low humidity and dryness.

Succulents

These plants are much more diverse than cacti. Some come from cactus areas but more come from the African continent and other parts of the world. While a few are hardy, like the houseleeks from the European mountains, and some sedums from various parts of the world, these groups are usually considered to be primarily alpines. Because most of these don't take kindly to a greenhouse environment, they are not so often grown by cacti collectors.

The majority of succulents can be split into three groups: leaf succulents, stem succulents, and "caudiciform" or root succulents. Their 10,000 or so different species occur in many different plant families and often not all species in a genus are succulent, such as Euphorbia. In many cases, it is often difficult to decide where succulence ends or begins. Probably the best definition of

Newly rooted succulent plant cuttings.

a succulent plant is "one usually found in a succulent plant collector's glasshouse."

The largest group are the leaf succulents and these are modified in different ways. Some have rosettes of thick, swollen, leathery leaves like the large growing Aloes and Agaves, sometimes on stems, sometimes flush with the ground. Smaller growing rosettes are found in the Echeverias from Mexico; these are popular for their often brightly colored leaves. The Crassula family are mostly bush forming, from tiny little clumping plants to larger and more majestic money or jade plants. These mostly have thick swollen leaves of different shapes, colors, and sizes. The other major group of succulent plants are the Mesembryanthemums or ice plants. This is a very large group that includes many bushy species with showy flowers, such as Lampranthus, which are often used in landscaping in frost-free areas. At the opposite end of the scale are the Conophytums, small clumping plants, whose plant body is composed of two almost united leaves, which rather resemble small peas. Between these are many differently shaped, usually low-growing plants, with slender or fat, chunky leaves all of which produce bright, daisy-like flowers.

The second major group are the stem succulents. These are often plants that to the uninitiated resemble cacti. The largest group are the Euphorbias from Africa and India. Some make leaves when in active growth, often minute, which are shed during periods of drought. Some grow to look like little bushes, others become tall and majestic like trees. A large number of different plant families have a few succulent members like the Baobab from East Africa.

The last group are those that are often referred to as "caudiciform," which usually includes those plants with swollen bases or subterranean large storage organs. These are generally much harder to cultivate, as the caudex is often prone to rotting if too wet, too humid or too cold. These forms also appear in many plant families such as the Cucumber family and Apocynaceae. Many of these plants produce slender, climbing, annual growth, which dies back during periods of drought.

PLANT CARE

With such a wide range of over 10,000 species, any care given can only be of a generalized nature. Where individual species differ widely in their requirements these will be given under that species.

Light   In general terms, plants need a bright position in which to grow well. In higher latitudes this will usually mean full sun but in lower ones small succulents may well burn up in constant full summer sun. For these types of plants, light shade will probably be beneficial.

In higher latitudes, many plants make ideal subjects for the window sill, but remember that when plants are placed 2–3 feet (60–90cm) from a window, the light level will be dramatically lower, perhaps around half. Most of these plants naturally come from a low humidity environment and therefore the dry heat of a modern house is ideal. In places that are not frost free, an outdoor structure such as a greenhouse will certainly give good results, provided that it can be heated to the minimum requirements.

In lower frost-free latitudes, a lathe house may provide the dappled shade required by some of the succulents. This structure can be open-sided for ventilation and covered in polythene during the rainy season.

Watering   Most cacti and succulents grow in the summer and require watering during that period. Ideally, plants should be given a good soaking with water and then allowed to dry out before watering again. For plants in large containers, sufficient water should be given at a time so that they dry out in about ten days.

When plants are at the bottom end of their temperature range in winter, they should be kept dry. In the height of summer, when excessive temperatures tend to make them go dormant, water sparingly. In higher northern latitudes, winter treatment usually starts about September/October and finishes about March. Any water given during this period should be little and infrequent, but this does very much

Cacti that favor growing in full sun are great for a window sill display.

depend on individual plants and the weather. Ideally during winter, plants should be allowed to go dormant and only sufficient water given to prevent any undue dehydration occurring.

In frost-free areas where plants can be permanently grown outdoors in beds, providing that a porous well-drained soil is used, larger established plants will probably require very little maintenance. In periods of drought, they will probably benefit from the occasional hosing down.

Temperature   Most cacti and succulent plants come from frost-free areas, or, where colder temperatures are found, it is usually extremely dry with a low humidity. For most general collections in higher latitudes, a good minimum safe temperature is about 50°F (10°C). At this temperature, most will be fairly trouble free. In glasshouses at temperatures lower than this, usually high humidity causes rot.

Some plants will tolerate these lower temperatures by a few degrees, but in a glasshouse the minimum safe temperature is usually about 44°F (16°C) as below this many plants will suffer with rot or disfigurement. The use of a circulatory fan will keep the air moving and help to reduce fungal infections.

Where plants can be safely grown outdoors in the lower latitudes, because of the longer and brighter days, many plants can tolerate the occasional short drop below these temperatures. It is the prolonged cold and damp that these plants will not tolerate.

Growing Medium   There must be as many suggestions for the right growing medium as there are cactus collectors. It is possible to grow these plants in anything from pure sand to pure clay, but the more extreme the more difficult it becomes. In different parts of the world, different material types are available locally, and these are usually used. The idea is to create an open, well-drained compost, but one that will also retain some moisture. This is usually achieved by using about one third grit or pumice and two thirds soil or a mixture of peat/coco fiber/or other similar ingredient, either with or without a soil-based compost. The compost should stay open when in use and not become hard and dense, as just pure garden soil tends to.

When plants are grown outdoors in permanent beds, it is a good idea to raise them above the surrounding ground level to allow for good drainage. The existing soil can be enhanced with some organic material to help retain some moisture and plenty of gravel to keep it open and allow for good drainage.

Cacti and succulents seem to be quite hungry plants and certainly grow better when well fed. They are slow-growing plants and therefore do not need high amounts of nitrogen, but seem to need all the major and minor elements. A good

Cacti make a magnificent focal point in a Texas landscape.

Cacti seedlings are growing beneath cuttings suspended above them.

Pocket Guide to Cacti and Succulents

base fertilizer should be added to any compost, one that has all the trace elements included. The acidity of the soil is also important. When the pH of the soil is either very low or very high, many of the elements turn into insoluble compound that are unavailable to the plants. The ideal pH value for most plants seems to be between 5.5–6.5, as, in this range, most of the elements in the soil are available to plants. Certain plants from calcareous regions also seem to need calcium in the soil. Usually with a lack of this, the plants develop a poor root system, and are therefore more difficult to grow. For many of the white-spined North American and Mexican cactus, together with some of the very slow growing ones like Ariocarpus, the addition of some chalk to the compost will be beneficial. This seems more important than changing the acidity of the compost.

PROPAGATION

It is great fun growing these plants and there is a great sense of achievement in taking a cutting or some seed and nurturing it along until it makes a beautiful flowering plant. As one gains experience, one hopes that each time another generation of plant grows it will be better than the last one, and often is. Plants raised under your own conditions from the beginning will not have to adapt from a change in environment.

Seed   This is probably the easiest way to grow new plants. There are many sources of seed throughout the world and they are comparatively cheap from people specializing in cacti and succulents. Most seed lists seem to come out during the winter months when there is time to go through them and select those plants you want to try. If you are not all that experienced, avoid very rare plants, as these are usually rare because they are awkward and difficult to grow.

If you have a propagator, wait until the days start to lengthen then sow them and keep them in a temperature of about 70°F (21°C) to 80°F (27°C) when most of

A close-up of cacti seedlings.

them will normally germinate in 2–4 weeks, although some can take six months. When they have germinated, they can be removed from the propagator and kept at a temperature of 50°F (10°C) and above, but out of full sun. Seed is best sown in small containers, with one type to a pot because they germinate and grow at different rates; this avoids the quicker growing ones swamping the slower ones. Fill the container with a gritty well-drained compost and lightly compact it. Carefully scatter the seed over the surface and cover this with a thin layer of fine course grit (not a rounded sand). Stand it in water about half the depth of the pot and allow it to soak for an hour or so until it becomes waterlogged. Place it in the propagator and do not allow it to dry out completely before germination has taken place.

If you do not have a propagator, wait until a little later in the year when seedlings can be placed on a window sill or in a greenhouse and nature will provide the heat needed.

Unless you have a particular reason for doing so, such as disease, the longer that you are able to leave the pots of seedlings alone, the better they will grow. It is virtually impossible to transplant very small seedlings without causing extensive damage to their root systems. Wait until the seedlings are at least pea-size, before handling them.

Cuttings The other main way of propagating some of these plants is by using cuttings. Hybrids and selected cultivars can only be propagated this way. The disadvantage of this method is that you can only take cuttings from something that you already have; this therefore does not enlarge your range of plants. If you require a large number of plants, then numerous stock plants are needed to provide the necessary amount of cuttings.

Some plants branch at soil level or offset making new

An old cut stem is beginning to branch out.

shoots, which will in some species produce a root system. The clump can then easily be divided to make more plants. After detaching the offsets, they should be allowed to dry for a period of a day or so until the point of attachment has calloused over. Where the offsets do not produce roots, these can still be detached with a knife and the cuttings and parent left exposed to the air until all the cut surfaces have produced a hard, calloused surface.

Bushy plants can also be cut back and the "prunings" from them used as cuttings. It is best to take comparatively short cuttings as otherwise they can collapse under their own weight during the rooting process.

A large old cutting branching from the areole.

Larger and thicker stems can also be severed and many of these will also root down, but more slowly than smaller cuttings. Larger cuttings must be allowed to callous over before being rooted. They should be placed in a warm, dry environment out of direct sun. Depending on temperature and time of year, this process can take from a week to a month or more.

Rooting cuttings   When the cuttings have calloused over, they are ready for rooting. Small cuttings are probably best rooted in shallow pots or trays (2–3 inches (5–7.5cm) deep). Larger cuttings should be rooted in the smallest pot that they will comfortably stand up in.

Small cuttings   Put a gritty, free-draining, cactus compost in the pots or trays within about an inch of the top of the container. Fill the pot with a thick layer of fine, coarse grit. It is better to keep cacti and succulents separate, as most succulents will root far more quickly. Shrubby succulent cuttings should simply be pushed through the grit into the compost, deep enough for them to stand up in it; rosettes should just be "screwed" into the surface of the grit. Their containers should be kept in a bright, airy, warm environment and kept slightly damp. The cuttings should normally root down in 2–6 weeks, although some species can be more obstinate.

When active new growth can be seen, it is usually an indication that the cuttings have rooted. Water the cuttings well and wait for a week. A gentle tug will soon tell you if they are rooted or not. The pots can then be tipped out and the new plants potted individually.

Larger cuttings   Take the smallest pot that the cutting will comfortably stand up in and fill about one-third of it full of gritty compost. Cover the surface with a thin layer of fine grit. Stand the cutting on the layer of grit and fill the rest of the pot with grit.

By keeping the compost damp, this method isolates the cutting from being in constant contact with wet soil, but still some moisture will rise and condense on

Kalanchoe "Fangs" being propogated from leaves.

the grit to provide the dampness that will encourage the cutting to produce roots without rotting. The amount of water given will be directly related to temperature and pot size, so that the compost is kept just damp rather than wet.

Larger cuttings can be much slower to root, taking perhaps 1–3 months or longer in some types of plants. When active new growth is seen, it is probably an indication that the cutting has started to root. Wait for about a month and then carefully tip the plant on its side and shake out the grit. If new roots can be seen, fill up the pot with compost and treat the plant normally for another month. The fresh roots on larger cuttings are often fine and easily damaged, even by repotting them.

You can have great fun in propagating plants by this method, but do it with a purpose; 327 plants of the same thing can be embarrassing if there is no room left to grow anything different.

PESTS AND DISEASES

Most cacti and succulent plants are not particularly susceptible to pests or diseases. Generally, the same insects that will attack other garden plants will also attack these plants. Growing them under the wrong conditions is the most common cause of diseases.

One particular pest that will attack cacti is the mealy bug. It is a small white creature that resembles a woodlouse. It is covered in a dense coating of wax and makes nests rather like little pieces of cotton wool. Because of its waxy coating, it tends to repel water (and insecticide), so the addition of a wetting agent (like soap) to a solution will help an insecticide to penetrate and work better. Persistence will eventually get rid of it.

Because of the modern trend for safer and safer chemicals, it is usually a case of checking with your supplier to find out what is currently available. From all those that we have tried over the years, applied as directed, none seem to be particularly detrimental to the plants. Avoid watering/spraying the plants in full sun so that there are not drops of hot insecticide sitting on them or this may cause spotting.

Having the plants in too high a humidity at too low a temperature causes most fungal or bacterial diseases. Plants are much more likely to rot from the bottom in wet and poorly drained compost. Rotting from the top can be a sign that the plants have been exposed to frost or too cold an environment for the species. Use a well-drained open compost and curtail watering at low temperatures. As above, check with your supplier for a suitable product to combat a specific problem.

Plant Directory

In this volume, I have tried to use the most recent names for the plants. Over the years many botanists have attributed names to plants, often in ignorance of what other botanists in different parts of the world were doing Some botanists looked for minute differences between species, while others looked for similarities. All of this led to a large surplus of names and made plant identification, with any degree of certainty, extremely difficult.

Over the last decade, the International Organisation for Succulent Plant Study, better known as the IOS, has fostered a new publication in eight parts, the *Illustrated Handbook of Succulent Plants*. While this work is probably too expensive for the average collector, it is a superb reference work, covering all succulents, including the cactus family. Although there are many name changes that are sure to upset specialists in particular groups, many similar species have been amalgamated, which makes it far simpler to identify individual species. In some species, which are now quite variable, probably collectors will want to use form names to differentiate collectable, different-looking plants.

The late Ted Anderson, who studied cacti for the last half century, eventually managed to publish the first major update of the cactus family since the 1920s (*The Cactus Family* by E. A. Anderson, Timber Press). Unfortunately he died shortly before its publication. Working with many of the world's leading cactus specialists, including the IOS, it embodies most of the changes envisaged at the time of writing. It is a superb, well-illustrated volume and a must for the keen cactus collector who wishes to identify plants. I have adopted these names here, although there are likely to be a few minor changes in due course.

Cacti growing in habitat in Arizona.

Cactus

x Aporophyllum, A. Beautie, A. Dawn, A. Edna Bellamy, A. Vivide

A. Beautie

This hybrid genus is derived from Aporocactus (now Disocactus) and the Epiphyllum hybrids. The long, slender, pendent stems of *Aporocactus flagelliformis* are maintained in this genus and combined with the type of flower associated with the Epiphyllum hybrids.

Disocactus flagelliformis has small trumpet-shaped flowers, either cerise or red, and flowers early in the year. This characteristic is also maintained in the hybrids, flowering between *D. flagelliformis* and the slightly later Epiphyllum hybrids.

These are ideal hanging-basket plants that make long pendent stems and, when grown well, give abundant flowers in spring, alongside the previous year's growth. Its flowers are mainly 3–5 inches (7.5–13cm) in diameter, and are mostly pink, orange, and red to purple. Although *D. flagelliformis* is remarkably tolerant of lower temperatures the hybrids will grow better in a warm, humid environment. During the winter, these plants will need the occasional light watering as otherwise the tips of the stems may die

A. Dawn

A. Edna Bellamy

back. During the spring and summer, the plants should be watered well and then allowed to almost dry before being watered again. Like many epiphytic cacti, they benefit from regular feeding during the spring and summer.

These plants like a bright situation, but not full summer sun. In a bright position, the stems will take on beautiful purple hues, which is a sign of good health.

There are numerous hybrids, but many are similar. Propagate named hybrids from cuttings or cross-pollinate with Epiphyllum hybrids and grow new hybrids from seed.

A. Vivide

Astrophytum asterias

Astrophytum are a small group of slow-growing cacti, mainly from Mexico. Most plants in this genus seem to require calcium in the soil; this can be easily added as ground chalk. It seems that without calcium these plants make a very poor root system and are much more difficult to grow.

Of all the species *A. asterias* is probably the most troublesome to grow, so many collectors prefer to graft their plants. The Japanese have hybridized this species to produce a large number of named cultivars with much more pronounced markings.

These small growing plants are rather like green mushrooms and pull themselves flat to the ground when they are dry. The plants flower during

A healthy plant requires some calcium in the soil.

Astrophytum asterias has a disk-like body.

the summer with quite large yellow flowers, often with a red base to the petals. The minimum safe temperature for them is 50°F (10°C) in winter and they need to be completely dry. Propagate from seed.

Astrophytum capricorne

This is another slow-growing member of this genus. Its small, globular bodies are usually covered with quite dense, soft, slender spines. These can vary in color from light brown to almost black. The body beneath may have the usual white flecks associated with Astrophytum but often they are lacking. The body is usually a dark olive green.

This species also has attractive bright yellow flowers, which are 2–3 inches (5–7.5cm) in diameter, and whose petals usually have red bases, making them look as if they have a red center.

The addition of calcium to the soil will help this species develop a good root system, and thereby will become easier to grow. This is not an easy species to grow and should be kept in full sun and dry in winter. Propagate from seed.

Astrophytum capricorne is covered in soft, curling spines.

Astrophytum myriostigma and v. nudum

Most plants of this species are comparatively small, globular-to-short, cylindrical plants usually densely covered in white flecks of minute spines. With very great age, these plants eventually become columnar in shape, but this takes many decades to happen.

A. myriostigma is a very variable species in the wild and there are many different forms in cultivation. Some are slender and columnar, while others are short and squat. Some give the appearance of gray plants; others have a distinct purple tinge to the plant body under dense white flecks. The number of ribs present is also extremely variable, ranging from three in the odd extreme example to about eight or nine at the other extreme. The more usual number is about five, but extra ribs can be produced or shed by any size of plants.

The green bodies and yellow flowers of v. *nudum*.

Flowers are produced regularly throughout the summer.

The plant is typically squat.

This species has much smaller flowers than the other members of this genus. They are a bright pale yellow, often 1–2 inches (2.5–5cm) in diameter, and produced regularly throughout the summer months.

As for the other members of this genus, add some ground chalk to the compost to improve its root system. Propagate from seed. Seedlings will flower when only an inch (2.5cm) or so in diameter, at about 3–4 years old.

This tall columnar specimen illustrates one of a range of different forms in cultivation.

Astrophytum ornatum

This is by far the easiest Astrophytum to grow and flower. It soon becomes columnar in shape and with great age can become a column more than 4 feet (1.2m) tall. Its flowers are bright yellow, 2–3 inches (5–7.5cm) in diameter, and produced regularly during the summer months.

These Astrophytums have spiney stems and larger flowers.

This is the only Astrophytum that has straight sharp spines and is sometimes hybridized with *A. myriostima* to make interesting and attractive plants. Often its seedlings, although at first glance resembling *A. myriostigma*, have very angular ribs and some straight spines.

Seed of this species usually germinates very quickly and many seedlings will flower when about three years old. This species responds well to feeding and will soon grow to make an extremely attractive plant.

Like the other forms of this species, it is not unusual to find specimens that either completely lack white flecks or only have a sparse covering.

Carnegia gigantea

The giant Saguaro is everybody's idea of the ideal cactus shape. Made famous in many cartoons and Western films, it is a native of Arizona south to northern Mexico.

This very tall-growing plant is also very slow, taking many years to reach a height of just one foot. It seems to have a very short growing season each year. During summer, it seems to grow for about six weeks and then stop, despite ideal conditions.

Many collectors and advertising agencies would love an adult plant about 3 feet (1m) tall, but unfortunately this species does not usually branch until it has reached 10 or more feet (3m) tall, a great age, and weighs several hundred pounds. Usually the only chance of obtaining a large cactus of this type is to get a tagged and authorized specimen from the Department of Agriculture, after it has been moved from its original habitat.

Still, this cactus is not difficult to grow from seed. Young plants look quite different from adult ones.

Carnegia gigantea in habitat.

Cephalocereus senilis

This is another of the tall-growing column cactus and is also very slow to grow. Specimens of about 50 years old can be about 6 feet (2m) tall.

It is not difficult to see why the common name for this plant is old man cactus.

These plants have a dense covering of long white hair that has led to the common name of old man cactus. Old cultivated plants are often discolored and dirty toward the base; these can be cleaned to some degree by spraying with warm soapy water and gently using a small brush. Growing them in full sun will often bleach out the remaining dirt to leave a more attractive plant.

Natives of Mexico, they need to be dry in winter or they are very prone to rot. During the summer, providing they are in well-drained compost, they will take normal watering and grow perhaps a half inch (1cm) or more a year.

When these plants reach 10–12 feet (3–4m) tall they are flowering size and begin to produce extra long, white wool down one side where the flowers appear from.

Cereus haageanus

The genus Cereus at one time contained most of the tall column cactus. As time progressed, however, botanists found small groups within the genus to have many similarities and these were subsequently divided into other genera. Cereus is now a comparatively small group of tall-growing, shrubby or tree-like plants that have funnel-shaped flowers at night.

This comparatively rare species from Paraguay has long, slender, almost square blue stems and was included in Monvillea. During the summer, it flowers freely in flushes, producing many whitish trumpet-shaped flowers from long lengths of its stems.

It is an easy plant to grow and soon bushes out, but normally needs some support as its stems become longer. This is one of the smaller flowering Cereus that will reliably flower most years. It has plenty of flowers produced in flushes several times a year and propagates easily from cuttings.

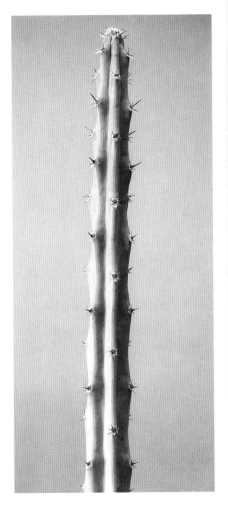

Cereus haageanus has a slender, clambering stem.

Cereus hildemannianus

This is now said to be the correct name for the plant that most people know as *Cereus peruvianus*. It has tall, blue-green, angular, poorly spined stems and when about 4 feet (1.2m) or more tall produces its large, whitish flowers at night at certain periods during the summer.

This plant is also well known for its monstrose form in which its stems become distorted, twisted, or lumpy, making a strongly architectural plant. The monstrose form is not as free flowering as the species.

There are many species similar to this one, with roughly similar shapes. However, this is

The monstrose form has unusual ribs.

probably the most hardy as many of the others are quite tropical and not tolerant of lower temperatures. In frost free areas this will make an ideal large feature plant in any garden. The monstrose form will also make an outstanding feature plant in a pot for any display.

Cereus hildemannianus usually has straight ribs.

The multi-branching stems of this monstrose form makes an attractive house plant.

Cleistocactus baumannii

Cleistocactus are in the main, slender-stemmed, bushy, or branching column cactus, that are widespread in South America. Recently, many other genera have been transferred to this genus, in particular most of the column cactus that were once classifed as Borzicactus. In the old genera, the flowers were tubular, just opening at the tips, but now some open more fully. The tubular shape of the flower retains nectar, which encourages humming birds to feed and pollinate them.

C. baumannii is a slender species, often branching at the base to make stems that are initially erect but later arch or become prostrate. The 2 inch (5cm) long, bright red flowers curve sharply upward.

Cleistocactus baumannii branches at the base.

This is a fairly variable species but is easy to grow, some forms flowering when quite young and small. These will often flower throughout the spring and summer months.

Cleistocactus ritteri

This species was described as *Cephalocleistocatus ritteri,* as it was one of a small group of Cleistocactus, which when they reached flowering size began to produce uneven long white, hair-like spines from the flowering zone. This feature is no longer considered significant and it has been transferred to Cleistocactus.

C. ritteri has slender, upright stems, closely covered in short, white spines. Its flowers are a bright canary yellow, an unusual color in this genus. This species will flower when about 2 feet (60cm) tall, and then flowers freely on and off during the summer months. It is a little sensitive to lower temperatures and a minimum of 45°F (7°C) is recommended.

Like most Cleistocactus, it will grow very much better in a deep pot that is large enough for it. Often, because of its narrow stem diameter, it is underpotted and starved. In a sunny position, with adequate food and water, it will grow quite quickly and produce more flowers.

This species has unusual yellow flowers.

Cleistocactus strausii

This is the most outstanding of the Cleistocactus. Its common name of silver
torch cactus is very appropriate for a well-grown specimen of this type. It is a
fairly quick-growing erect column cactus, flowering when about 2–3 feet
(60–90cm) tall. It needs a reasonable-
sized, full depth pot and moderate
amounts of food and water during the
summer months. It also seems quite tolerant of low temperatures during winter,
providing it is dry.

The common name for this plant is silver torch cactus.

This species is often under potted
by cactus collectors, who fail to realize
the beauty of a well-grown specimen.
When it is grown poorly, its main stem
has a tendency to go blind when about
1–2 feet (30–60cm) tall and it begins to
offset until it becomes a very thin multi-
stemmed plant. Its stems usually look
tired and are often discolored.

Compare this with a well-grown
silver-white spined plant. Its stems are
probably twice the diameter and will
grow to about 6 feet (2m) tall, branching from the base only occasionally. An old
plant that has been looked after will produce stems 3–4 inches (7.5–10cm) in
diameter and hundreds of flowers during the spring. Stems that have grown too
tall can be removed lower down and the plant will produce several new branches
in its place. These cut stems can be dried and made into cuttings.

Cleistocactus winteri (Hildewinteria aureispina or Borzicactus aureispinus)

For flowers, this must be the most rewarding of all the Cleistocactus. From cuttings, it will flower when about 9 inches (23cm) long, and on and off from spring until the autumn will produce star-like, orangey red flowers. This plant is slender-stemmed, and

Cleistocactus winteri is better known as *Hildewinteria aureispina* or *Borzicactus aureispinus*.

densely covered in golden, short, bristly spines. Its stems are initially erect but later arch over and, if in contact with soil, will root down to make large mounds. Medium-sized plants of this type are often likened to an octopus. This is a fairly easy plant to grow from seed, flowering at about three to four years old.

This plant makes numerous long, arching stems. After several years, these will discolor and eventually die back, so each year prune to remove any tired looking stems low down. Its base will soon branch out and make several new ones.

Copiapoa cinerea

This very old plant has grown about 1 inch (2.5cm) in 20 years.

This fascinating genus of plants from the northern coastal plain of Chile is very much a mystery. Chile's coastal plane rarely receives any rain, perhaps just a few millimeters every ten years. From records there seems to have been little change in the weather for the last 400 years. Along the coast flows the cold Humbolt current, which brings thick fog and mists; it is from these that the plants receive what moisture they are able to obtain. These fogs do not progress very far inland and the plants are mostly found close to the coast.

Needless to say, these plants are very slow-growing and according to the ardent enthusiasts who have visited the same areas over the decades, plants of this kind seem to grow very little if at all. This is not surprising, except that there are some clumping plants that are 6–10 feet (2–3m) or more in diameter; how old these are nobody knows.

It seems that the more that you know about this group of plants, the more confusing it all becomes. In many places several different species grow, and if you progress through their habitats and compare them you will find that their forms gradually change. Seedlings take many years to develop adult characteristics so that the picture becomes even more confused. It has been mooted that there is only one species that is variable. On the other hand, there are currently about 20 recognized species. These fit into four or five different groups, but even these merge into each other. *Copiapoa cinerea* is one of the most spectacular. It has large, gray heads with straight spines like little telegraph poles marching toward the crown. These can be a beautiful black color or lighter. It is extremely slow-growing taking several decades to reach the size of a small melon. In the wild, some of the large clumps of these cacti have 200 or more heads! Several similar species (or forms) exist, and these are probably closely related.

Copiapoa krainziana

The dense white spines on this species make it an extremely beautiful plant when cultivated. It is now considered to be a long-spined variant of *Copiapoa cinerea*.

Dense white spines are a particular feature of this plant.

Copiapoa mollicula

Quite a number of smaller growing, globular plants are ribbed and spiny with erect, short, stiff spines. Like many of this group, different plants have been typified by different authors, even cacti from the same general habitat,

A typical climbing plant.

leading to confusion as to which is the "genuine" *Copiapoa mollicula*. Even if this problem can be resolved, the question then arises, is it just variable or are the others different species? Whatever name is chosen makes little difference to the plant, so from a cultivation point of view, if it looks different, and you like it, it is worth growing. Keep in mind, however, that juvenile and adult plants often look quite different. There is little to differentiate the flowers of any species in this group, as they are all yellow, some lighter and some darker.

Copiapoa tenuissima

There is another small distinctive group of Copiapoas that have little dark chocolate-colored plant bodies, which grow to just a few inches in diameter, usually fairly close to the ground and often offsetting to make clumps. There are several species in this group, which are all fairly similar, but this is a distinctive species with short, even spines, often fairly dense. Plants flower when just two to three years old from seed at about one inch (2.5cm) in diameter.

The more that people study this genus of plants and they check and cross-reference early descriptions, the more confused they become. Find a dozen specialists of this group, present a plant, and be prepared for them to come up with twelve different names!

A chocolate colored body with a woolly crown makes this plant distinctive.

Coryocactus erectus

This genus of shrubby to tree-like plants from western South America now includes the old genus Erdisia. There is much confusion about the naming of this group and currently there are thought to be about a dozen species in it. Many

This plant has tall stems and flowers from the tip.

are slender-stemmed, branching plants, which soon become top heavy and lean over, making large mounds of plants.

C. erectus is slender-stemmed and, although initially erect, soon leans or arches over to the ground. The slender stems produce large, bright orange flowers at their tips during the summer months. This species has perhaps a bad choice of Latin name, as it is not a particularly erect plant.

It is an easy plant to grow and its older, unwieldy stems can be removed from time to time to make a more compact plant. The top 9–12 inches (23–30cm) of the old stems can be made into cuttings and several planted together in a pot will soon make an attractive new plant. Keep in mind that flowers are only produced near the tips of the stems, so it is best to cut the plants back in late summer so that you do not remove all of this year's flowers.

Coryphantha pallida

This widespread genera of North American cactus is closely related to Mammillaria. The main characteristic that separates it from others is the groove in the upper side of its tubercle. The problem is that not all Coryphantha seem to have this, and some only have it on large old plants. Most are globular to shortly cylindrical plants, which offset to make clumps and often with a swollen tuberous root. Their flowers are mostly yellow and open during the day. Some flowers have a red center and a few species have pink flowers.

The most recent research has done little to help solve the taxonomy of this group. Some species are very variable, others have juvenile and adult forms, and a lot more research needs to be done before a firm classification system can be formed.

C. pallida is initially solitary but later clusters to make clumps. Its tubercles are close set, short, and thick. Its radial spines are golden but its central spines are almost black and curved. It produces yellow flowers 2–3 inches (5–7.5cm) wide in summer. This plant is normally propagated from seed.

Large, golden flowers are typical of this genus.

Coryphantha radians

This species is often solitary and grows slightly columnar with age. Its dense spination is pale yellow and usually without central spines. Like all Coryphanthas, the large yellow flowers, often up to about 3 inches (7.5cm) in diameter, are produced in the crown of the plant.

Like many of the Coryphanthas, these plants produce thickened tuberous roots, which can often fill small pots fairly quickly. As a result, their tops fail to grow larger. Although it does not, at first glance, appear that these plants need to be repotted, this should be done on a regular basis. It is only when these plants are taken out of their pots that the need for this becomes apparent. Repotting into a larger pot will usually spur the plants into a new burst of growth and many more flowers.

These cacti set seed fairly easily and make bright green seedpods in the crown, which look rather like small stretched grapes. These plants are normally propagated from seed.

Coryphantha radians forms multi-headed clumps.

Disocactus flagelliformis

Several of the old genera of epiphytic cacti have been reclassified into this genus. This species will be far better known as *Aporocactus flagelliformis*. It is one of the parents of the hybrid genus x *Aporophyllum*.

This species from Mexico has slender, cylindrical, creeping or pendent stems. These are quite densely spined with short, softish golden spines. The small beak-like flowers are produced early in the spring. The flowers usually associated with this species are a bright pink to cerise, but another form with slightly less spined stems and red flowers is also cultivated, the old *A. flagriformis*.

Plants of this species make ideal hanging basket plants and, grown well, the stems can reach up to more than 6 feet (2m) in length. During the winter, if dry, these plants seem to be able to tolerate temperatures down to almost freezing for short periods. If they are grown at higher temperatures, then they will need very little water during winter as otherwise the tips of the stems will tend to die back.

For a good show of flowers, feed it well during the summer and grow it in a bright position, but not full summer sun.

Bright flowers are produced early in the year.

Disocactus martianus

This old Aporocactus has much more robust stems than *D. flagelliformis*. They are stiff and pendent, and covered in golden spines. It was suggested at one time that this was a Cleistocactus. The 2–3 inch (5-7.5cm) long flowers are almost straight and a bright red in color. It is not as free-flowering as *D. flagelliformis*, producing its flowers from time to time during the summer.

It is best grown in a hanging basket so that its stems can hang down. The oldest stems gradually become discolored and each year in spring, this plant should be tidied and any old and unsightly growth should be removed. The decent cuttings can be rooted to make new plants. Most of the epiphytic cactus naturally clamber in the wild, tending to root down as they go. When grown in pots, they eventually become very woody at the base and are best started again perhaps every ten years or so.

This species is normally propagated from cuttings.

Disocactus martianus has long pendent stems.

Disocactus phyllanthoides

Another recent addition to this genus, *Disocactus phyllanthoides* was previously correctly known as *Nopalxochia phyllanthoides*. It was also cultivated as *Epiphyllum* Deutshe Kaiserin, which was just a selected cultivar of the species.

Bright pink flowers follow the pink buds.

This has been a very popular plant with its comparatively small pink flowers. The real advantage of this species is that the buds start to turn pink from a very small size, staying that color until the flowers open. This gives the impression of a very long flowering period. Often these plants flower so prolifically that their stems are completely used up and should be removed as they gradually wither.

This has been a very popular parent of some of the Epiphyllum hybrids, for its numerous small flowers and colorful buds. It is a little more cold-sensitive than some of the other Epiphyllum-like plants and will benefit from a winter temperature of about 50°F (10°C).

Disocactus speciosus f. amecamensis

The bright white flowers of this form make it unusual.

Yet another recent addition to this genus, this is one of a small group of angular, slender stemmed epiphytes previously known as Heliocereus. Most of this species have bright red flowers, quite large in some of them, and thought to be the parents of many of the early Epiphyllum hybrids.

D. speciosus does not like low temperatures and really needs at least 50°F (10°C) in winter to do well. The 5–7 inch (12–17cm) diameter flower is short-lived and has a fuchsine overtone, giving it an almost "bluish" tint to the red. This characteristic can be seen in many of these hybrids.

The form *amacamensis* is even more sensitive to cold than the species and needs an extra couple of degrees in winter. The flowers are produced toward the ends of the pendent stems several times during the summer. Unlike the species, they are white; the most shining white possibly seen on any cactus.

Echinocactus grusonii

The name Echinocactus was at one time used as a name for most of the cacti that were neither the tall column plants nor prickly pear. Over the years most have been split out to new genera, or groups of similar plants.

Echinocactus grusonii is commonly known as the golden barrel cactus, or mother-in-laws-seat. It is a large growing species, up to about 4 feet (1.2m) tall and up to 3 feet (1m) wide. It is more often grows with a single head in the wild but in cultivation, with better growing conditions, it will sometimes offset to make large clumps. In the wild this plant has become almost extinct.

While this species will grow fairly quickly during summer if grown in a rich compost, it is fairly sensitive to cold and needs a minimum temperature of 50°F (10°C) in winter to avoid it any marks appearing or any rotting occurring. It should be kept dry in winter as it seems prone to rotting if damp.

This plant will produce small, straw-colored flowers throughout the summer when it reaches 12–15 inches (30–38cm) in diameter. In higher latitudes it

The common name for *Echinocactus grusonii* is golden barrel cactus.

can take 50 years for this plant to achieve this size. In lower latitudes, with a frost free environment and good cultivation, the same size can probably be achieved in ten years.

Propagating the plant from seed is easy, providing the seedlings are not kept wet or at low temperatures.

Echinocactus platyacanthus

This is a large-growing, barrel cactus, that can reach perhaps up to about 8 feet (2.5m) tall and three feet (1m) or more in diameter. It has quite large, straight central spines, often arranged in a cross, which become black with age. Its radial spines are much shorter and often curved, although the spination in this species is quite variable.

There were a number of similar species of Echinocactus and these have now been made synonymous with this species. It is a slow-growing species and seedlings normally have a grayish color, which is quite distinctive.

This cactus has a slow-growing, gray plant body.

Echinocereus coccineus

The bright cup-like flowers of *Echinocereus coccineus*.

This large group of North American cacti extends south to northern Mexico and Baja, California. It is extremely popular with cactus collectors and has many species that are reputed to be hardy. Most are clumping plants with heads from one inch (2.5cm) diameter to large clumps with short columnar heads up to a foot (30cm) or more long. In habitat many species grow to become massive clumps and are usually quite widespread. There are many common names for each individual species, but perhaps hedgehog cactus is one that applies best to many. This genera has buds that develop inside the stems of the plants and are forced through the skin, which splits slightly to accommodate this. They also have green stigmas, the female part in the center of the flower. This can be various shades of green, and some are a much more yellowish green than others.

E. coccineus now embodies many old species. They are smaller-headed, clumping plants that in the wild will often make clumps up to about 3 feet (1m) in diameter. The flowers are often small in relation to the plant, 1–2 inches (2.5–5cm) in diameter, although they can grow to

The flowers of *Echinocereus coccineus* are very variable in color.

over 3 inches (7cm) in some forms. They are mostly in the orange to red spectrum, although shades of pink and violet are not uncommon.

In the wild these plants are closely related to *E. triglochidatus* and, in some areas, will hybridize with them.

These plants are easy to grow from seed and many will flower when only 3–4 inches (7–10cm) in diameter or less. Their funnel-shaped flowers last for several days. With all the synonyms that apply to it, this is now an extremely variable species.

Echinocereus pectinatus

This and the other closely related species are perhaps the most beautiful of the genus. They have a dense covering of short comb-like spines that completely obscure the plant body. At different times of the year, these spines change color, creating bands of colorful spines. This has given rise to the common name of rainbow cactus.

Numerous forms of this species exist and it seems almost as if every different habitat has its own variations. The spines on this type of cactus can vary completely in color from plant to plant. At the extreme, they can be black or white, but shades of orangy-red to brown are more usual.

In general, the Echinocereus with its dense pectinate spines is much slower-growing than other species.

The bands of colorful spines gave *Echinocereus pectinatus* its common name of rainbow cactus.

They are more of a challenge to grow, as they seem to have a much shorter growing season and are more prone to rotting at low temperatures. Propagate it from seed for a variety of different forms.

Echinocereus pentalophus

This species is very similar to *E. cinerascens*. Its flowers are similar in shape and color but a little smaller with stems that are much more slender. Its spination is also extremely variable, but its stems are still clearly visible through the spines.

This species can be propagated from cuttings but is easy to grow from seed. Seedlings will usually flower when three to four years old and can be grown in quite small pots.

Echinocereus pentalophus has large flowers in spring.

Echinocereus scheerii and v. gentryi

The flowers of *Echinocerus scheerii* open fully at night.

Plants of this species have slender, rigid stems that spread across the ground. Most are only lightly spined and *v. gentryi* only has very short spines, or is almost spineless in the form *cucumis*.

These plants flower freely in the spring with wine glass shaped flowers, often starting to open in the evening and fully during the night. During the day they tend to partially close. The flowers are about 2 inches (5cm) in diameter, usually orangey-pink, but red and pink forms also exist. The *v. gentryi* tends to have pinker flowers, which gradually turn orangey as the flowers mature. Flowers of this species last for several days and are usually produced over a period of time.

As the buds on Echinocereus are forced through the skin of the plant, dead flowers and ripe seed pods should be carefully removed as any rot on either can easily enter the plant's body and cause stem rot.

The flowers of *Echinocereus* v. *gentryi,* when open, are salmon pink and turn an orangey-pink color as they mature.

Echinopsis aurea

The genera Echinopsis has been greatly enlarged in recent years and some cynics say that soon all south American cacti will end up in this group! Historically, globular plants with very long flower tubes produced at night were classified as Echinopsis. The tall-growing column plants with long tubes flowers produced at night were Trichocereus. Globular plants with short-tubed, daytime flowers were termed Lobivia. Globular plants with long-tubed day flowers were Pseudolobivia.

As time progressed, more and more intermediate plants were discovered. These have now all been amalgamated, together with some other small genera. It is thought that several other major groups could also be incorporated under this name.

Echinopsis aurea is a day-flowering species that has been included in both Lobivia and Echinopsis. It is a small, columnar spiny plant with bright yellow flowers. Quite variable, it also has some other color forms. It is easy to grow and a useful plant as a pollen donor in the production of hybrids.

Bright yellow flowers are typical of this species.

Echinopsis backebergii f. winteriana

Lobivia was originally a large group of species that various botanists tried to reconcile over the years to make a sensible classification system. Since Lobivia has now become synonymous with Echinopsis, further amalgamations have been made, making workable identification possible.

Formerly a Lobivia, this species is quite variable. These plants have small heads that range from globular to short cylindrical, and often offset to make large clumps. The flowers are small, opening during the day and are short lived. They are mostly shades of orange to red and have a white throat.

This form produces beautiful pink flowers.

These are easy plants to grow. They easily flower and many are fairly tolerant of low temperatures. Propagate them by dividing the clumps, as the heads are often already rooted, or they can be grown from seed.

The form *winteriana* is a little less tolerant of cold and has delicate pink flowers.

Echinopsis candicans

This plant is quite robust and can tolerate the occasional drop in temperature.

This clumping species can grow to over a yard across. Its thick, chunky stems can reach a diameter of about 5 inches (12cm) and grow to about 2 feet (60cm) long. It is well armed with long golden brown spines. In cultivation in a glasshouse, it seems a little shy of flowering and is grown more for its general appearance. If you can flower it, they are 5–7 inches (12–18cm) wide, white produced at night, and sweetly scented.

In frost-free areas, this would make an ideal bedding plant, as it is quite robust and does not seem to mind the occasional low temperature, if dry.

It is easily grown from seed, and larger plants can be divided or some of its offsets removed. Like many of the clumping species, old heads can begin to look tired and are probably best removed from time to time to allow the new growth to fill in and rejuvenate the plant.

Echinopsis chamaecereus

A small-growing and clumping species with long, slender, trailing stems much better known under its old name of *Chamaecereus silvestrii*, it was originally cultivated in Argentina. It has never been found in the wild. When classified, it was transferred to Lobivia with which it will hybridize, but now, like all Lobivias, it is included in Echinopsis.

These plants are quite tolerant of low temperatures, surviving near freezing temperatures or below if completely dry. During the summer, they need quite a lot of water and feeding to make them grow well. Well-grown plants freely produce small, bright red flowers during spring and summer.

Such plants make a mass of stems, which are very lightly attached to their

Typical trailing stems of the red-flowered peanut cactus.

The flowers of the hybrid 'Jubilee.'

parent stem and make large mounds. Sometimes they can become detached from their parent and therefore fail to swell up when water is available. If this is a problem, then it is best to examine the plant and remove the offending bits. If you put three to four of these stems together in a small pot and keep them slightly damp, they usually root down very quickly and make an "instant" new plant.

In recent years, there have been numerous hybrids of this species produced, mostly by crossing it with other Lobivias. Most have trailing stems of different diameters, and spination and a variety of flower colors is possible.

The hybrid 'Jubilee' is a good example of a purple-flowered form. It is a little more compact than the species normally is, and has chunkier stems, which flower prolifically in summer.

It is best to grow these plants in a wide pan, as they soon reach the edge and cascade down over the rim. Because the stems are so weakly attached, care needs to be taken when repotting them, as they are prone to falling apart.

Echinopsis huasha and hybrids

This clumping species with cylindrical stems about 2–3 inches (5–7cm) in diameter grows to about 3 feet (1m) tall. Its stems, although initially erect, are not rigid enough to support the weight of the length to which they grow and tend to become prostrate, turning up at the tips. These plants offset freely to make large clumps, which helps to support the stems.

This species is more commonly seen with red or yellow flowers but there are all kinds of shades in between. Larger clumps will flower prolifically in summer. Although it is an easy plant to grow, it does seem prone developing black marks on the older stems. On a small plant, these can be quite noticeable but not so much so on a large clump. These marks are caused by a fungal infection, which seems quite localized and does not seem to affect the plant. Presumably growing these plants at a higher temperature would solve this problem.

There are many hybrids of these plants, which generally have a slightly more robust form with brightly colored flowers. Both the species and the hybrids are large clump-forming plants and would be very suitable for landscaping in frost-free areas.

These large bright flowers only last a day.

Echinopsis marsoneri

The bright day flowers of an old Lobivia.

This is now the correct name for many of the old Lobivias with globular to short cylindrical stems, usually solitary, with grayish-green plant bodies. Their flowers are mostly orange to red with a dark throat and are relatively large at 2–3 inches (5–7cm) in diameter.

Probably three of the best-known old species included in this group are *Lobivia glauca*, *L. haageana*, and *L. jajoiana*. These are all relatively slow-growing small species, which produce flowers from time to time during the summer.

These plants are quite variable and well worth cultivating, both for their attractive and distinctive body color and large flowers.

Although these are short-lived, their dark centers make an attractive combination with the petal color. This species is normally propagated from seed and will probably still be found under numerous old names.

Echinopsis maximilliana

An extremely variable, clump-forming species, its stems are about 2 inches (5cm) in diameter and grow to about a foot (30cm) long, often trailing along the ground. They are mostly straight-ribbed, but their spination is extremely variable. This group is another amalgam of a number of old Lobivia species. Its flowers are mostly reddish with yellow to orange throats and are 2–3 inches (5–7cm) long.

This species tends to be untidy in its growth pattern and often its old stems become quite marked. It is a good idea to propagate this species from cuttings every few years to start a new plant. Although it is a very variable species regarding its stem and spination, relatively long trailing stems and flower throat color are its distinguishing features.

Many of its different forms will still be found around under their old Lobivia names. These can be easily grown from seed.

One of the slender trailing stemmed species.

Echinopsis obrepanda

Many of the old species of Pseudolobivia now make up this species.

These plants are often solitary, some making small clumps as they age. The bodies are usually depressed at the crown, making them squat plants. Their bodies are often a glossy dark green and can be relatively large, up to about 8 inches (20cm) in diameter. Spination can be weak or strong, long or short, but is often parallel with the plant's body. Despite the size of the plant's body, they pro-

duce long-tubed flowers from about 4–8 inches (10cm–19cm) long, which are sometimes white but often in shades of pink to lavender.

This plant produces large flowers, relative to the size of its body.

Echinopsis tubiflora

One of the most robust of all the cacti is this good old Echinopsis. It has been in cultivation for well over a century and until recently was often thought to be mostly hybrids. Some recent collections of *E. oxygona* and *E. tubiflora* have proven to be almost exact matches of those that have been cultivated for years.

These two species offset very freely in cultivation, making large clumps. The offsets, which usually look totally different to the parent when small, are easily detached and root readily. It is much easier to propagate by this method rather than from seed. The plants themselves are very tolerant of long periods of neglect or drought, and also will tolerate low temperatures, if kept completely dry.

This is the crested form.

Perhaps one of the disadvantages of these two species is that they are almost indestructible, which has led some people to believe that cacti do not need water, food or care to make them grow. If only they could see how different these plants look when cared for.

Both species are very variable and have very long, tubed flowers that open in the evening and last about 24 hours. Both species are variable, but *E. tubiflora* has an almost white flower and *E. oxygona* has a pinkish one. These species are the principal parents for the following hybrids.

Echinopsis hybrids

E. oxygona and *E. tubiflora* are very easy to grow and produce beautiful, long, tubed flowers, up to about 10 inches (25cm) long and 4 inches (10cm) wide.

Echinopisis x Gay Firecracker

Unfortunately, the two old species that have been most popular are either white or shades of pink. In more recent times, various collectors have hybridized these with other species to make smaller growing plants, day-flowering plants, and a wide variety of different colors.

Echinopsis aurea has been used to introduce yellow flowers (such as in *Echinopsis* x Green Gold) and to produce shades of salmon to orange. Some of the old Lobivias, like *L. arachnacntha* with its bright red flowers, have also been used to make smaller growing plants and to add more color variants. Many of the Lobivia crosses have smaller flowers, but some of these open during the day rather than at night. The old Pseudolobivias, like *E. obrepanda,* have provided some of the deep pinks and other shades. There are also many other species that have been used to pro-

duce hybrids, which can be crossed to create a much wider range of colors—although they are very unpredictable from seed.

In frost-free areas where these plants can be grown outdoors in beds, they can be quite spectacular with large clumps producing batches of numerous flowers several times a year. One large outdoor display, for example, has plants that have been graded according to their color, creating an effect like a rainbow when they all flower. No decent collection should be without at least one of these plants. Good cultivation makes it a spectacular plant.

Echinopsis x Green Gold.

Epiphyllum anguliger

The Epiphyllum species all have flat stems that rather resemble leaves. Although some are short, many make long strap-like leaves. These plants are epiphytes, and can be found growing in trees where some humus has collected. The stems tend to clamber along branches, rooting where they touch, or to hang down. In

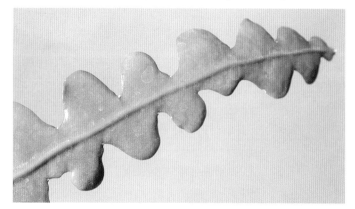

The unusual rick-rack stem of this plant.

the tropical jungles of Central America, these plants have adapted this form to capture light, as moisture conservation is of less importance. Most plants of this kind are night flowering, and often have very long, tubular flowers.

Most of the species prefer a higher winter temperature, minimum 50°F (10°C), as at lower ones they are prone to either marking badly or just rotting.

Epiphyllum anguliger, which has several synonyms, is a smaller, growing species with stems up to about one foot (30cm) long. It is comparatively narrow and its margins are heavily scalloped, sometimes right to the thickened and prominent mid-rib. Its flowers are small, 1–2 inches (2.5–5cm) in diameter, and highly scented. They are produced from time to time during the summer months in the evening and last for up to about 24 hours.

Epiphyllum hybrids

There are thousands of registered hybrid of Epiphyllum and probably twice that number of non registered ones. The first hybrids were produced in the 1800s and many people in different parts of the world have been producing new ones ever since.

Although the original hybrids were Epiphyllum species crossed with other genera, they have now been transferred to Selinicereus and Disocactus. These hybrids have then been crossed so that the parents of many of the new hybrids are a complete mystery.

Ephiphyllum x Ackermanni

For many years there were no yellow hybrids, as there did not appear to be any related species with yellow flowers. There were cream ones, but not a yellow one. Eventually a cross was made between *Echinopsis aurea* (pollen donor) and an Epiphyllum, and the first yellowish hybrid was produced. Over the years, these have been improved (like Clarence Wright and Queen Anne). Most of the yellow hybrids that are capable of producing intense yellow flowers will often produce white flowers with a hint of yellow, particularly when young.

An interesting recent discovery has been *Echinopsis* (*Trichocereus*) *arboricolus*, which is an epiphytic Echinopsis. A quick glance at the flowers of the old Trichocereus and Epiphyllum will show that they are similar in appearance. Now it is thought that *E. arboricolus* is possibly a link between these two genera.

Hybrids are generally easy to grow, but this does depend on the parents of the cross. Most of the old hybrids seem more robust than some of the newer

Epiphyllum x Clarence Wright.

ones. Older hybrids will tolerate temperatures down to near freezing for short periods, if kept quite dry. Many of the newer ones have a much greater affinity with Disocactus and these seem to need a minimum temperature of about 50°F (10°C).

These plants like a bright position but should be kept out of full summer sun, and possibly shaded throughout the year in lower latitudes. They should be watered well during the growing season and then watered again as they become dry. They will benefit from a low nitrogen fertilizer that is rich in all the other elements. When such plants are grown under very

Epiphyllum x Moonlight Sonata.

tropical conditions, it seems that these natural conditions act like a high nitrogen fertilizer that can stop them from flowering. Usually the addition of all the trace elements will correct this.

The flowers of the Epiphyllum hybrids are mostly in the region of 5–8 inches (13–20cm) in diameter, although there are some small flowered ones and a few

Epiphyllum x Giant Empress

hybrids with flowers over 12 inches (30cm) in diameter. Flowers vary in color from white to yellow to red and fuchsine with various levels of intensity.

Epiphyllum x Queen Anne

Eriosyce subgibbosa

The long trailing stem of ssp. *clavata*.

Eriosyce is a name that is unfamiliar to most cactus collectors. It is far better known under its old name of Neoporteria and its relatives. While it may be some time before collectors adopt the new name, the old one has sorted out many anomalies.

There used to be numerous genera and a multitude of species which were almost impossible to identify with any degree of certainty. Kattermann, in his revision of the genus has sorted out many of these problems with the groups of very similar plants now sharing the same name. Because there are so many changes, it is not just a case of changing Neoporteria to Eriosyce, as specific names have also been changed.

These plants from Chile and Argentina are mostly small slow-growing plants that come from very arid conditions. Most are solitary in habit, although a few will offset with age. Although the plants are initially globular, many will become cylindrical with age. Most of their flowers are small and different species flower at different times of the year.

E. subgibbosa has small, pink, tubular flowers whose petal tips open out. These flowers are usually produced from autumn to spring.

Espostoa lanata

These mostly Peruvian column plants are usually covered in dense white spines when in cultivation. Some species can be tree-like, others bushy, and with great age they can grow into large specimens. When plants reach flowering size, 3–4 feet (90–120cm) or more depending on species, they begin to produce tubular to bell-shaped flowers at night in summer. The flowering zone is modified to produce a lateral cephalium, which is an area covering several ribs, of dense often long and soft hair like spines. This rather resembles a beard on one side of the stem.

Espostoa lanata in cultivation is slow-growing and a large plant is probably only 3–4 feet (90–120cm) tall. In the wild, these may grow to 20 feet (6m) tall, branching in the upper parts. The dense white spines are fairly short, giving the plant a very neat appearance. Like most Espostoa,

Espostoa lanata has tall woolly stems.

these plants are very prone to rotting if kept at low temperatures in winter, particularly if they are wet. Propagation is usually from seed, but it takes many years to grow a specimen-sized plant.

Espostoa melanostele

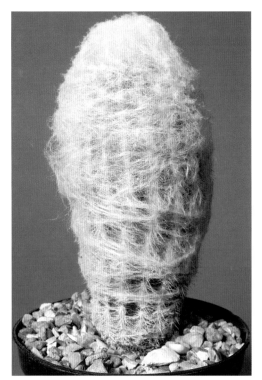

This plant is slow growing and has distinctive woolly stems.

This is a short species, growing up to about 6 feet (2m) tall with thicker stems that reach 5 inches (13cm) in diameter. The stems are densely covered in long, white, hair-like spines, resembling a plant covered in cotton. Some plants produce irregular, long, golden spines, which protrude through the white spines.

This is another slow growing species but one of the most beautiful. Often comparatively small plants will begin to offset and produce multiple stems. Like most Espostoa it is not tolerant of low temperatures or winter water.

Like many plants with woolly white spines, these can become discolored with pollution. Plants can often be cleaned to some degree by spraying with a high-pressure spray gun containing warm soapy water. Soak the plant well and leave for a little while for the dirt to soften then spray again. Particularly dirty plants may need repeat cleanings. Growing these plants in full sun will also help to bleach out any remaining dirt.

Espostoa senilis

Better known under its old name of *Thrixanthocereus senilis*, this species has fairly slender tall growing stems densely covered in short white spines. It is an extremely attractive plant and branches from the lower stems to make a bush.

The plants reach flowering size at about 4–5 feet (1.2–1.5m), when they start to make their lateral cephalium. It produces bright pink-purple flowers at night during the summer.

This species seems to tolerate temperatures down to 45°F (7°C) without problems, provided that it is dry.

Although this plant can be grown from cuttings, it is normally propagated from seed.

These are tall, densely spined plants. The cactus (left) shows the flowering zone.

Ferocactus cylindraceus

Barrel cacti are natives of the southern U.S.A. and Mexico. Many are large grow-ing plants and a prominent feature of the landscape.

Ferocactus cylindraceus is probably better known under its old name of

This species can have red or yellow spines.

F. acanthodes. It is a fairly slow-growing plant, yet it can reach about 9 feet (3m) tall and about two feet (60cm) in diameter. It is usually solitary and has long, stout ,twisted fish-hook spines. Like all Ferocactus, the yellow flowers are produced near the crown on mature plants.

Most of the larger-growing Ferocactus will benefit from regular repotting to speed up growth. They will do best in a half-depth pot with regular feeding dur-ing the spring and summer. Although these plants require moderate amounts of water in the summer, they are quite prone to rotting in winter if kept damp.

Ferocactus echidne

This is one of the smaller-growing type of barrel cactus, which can reach about 18 inches (45cm) tall and 12 inches (30cm) in diameter. It is one of the less spiny species and has straight golden-brown spines.

This species flowers when quite small.

One of the advantages of this species, apart from its tolerance to lower temperatures, is that it will flower when small, about 4 inches (10cm) in diameter. Its yellow flowers are 1–2 inches (2.5–5cm) in diameter and produced from time to time during the summer months. Like most Ferocactus, these are normally propagated from seed. A few of the smaller-growing species will flower after about 5 years when grown from seed.

Ferocactus glaucescens

This cactus has a large blue-green body and golden spines.

This attractive species has a distinct blue-green plant body and awl-shaped golden spines. It grows to 1–2 feet (30–60cm) tall and is about the same in diameter. It frequently offsets to make clumps. It produces comparatively small, yellow flowers, during the early summer.

F. glaucescens grows at a reasonable speed but requires a minimum temperature of at least 50ºF (10ºC) in winter. At lower temperatures, it marks badly or, even worse, small plants will rot.

This species makes an attractive feature plant in a half-depth pot or half barrel. In frost-free areas, these look beautiful when planted as a colony.

Ferocactus histrix

A medium-sized species, this grows up to about 3 feet (1m) in diameter and height. Plants of this type have 20–40 ribs and spines up to about 3 inches (7cm) long. With the comparatively large number of ribs and long straight spines, which are often banded in color, this is a fairly distinctive species. Small yellow flowers are produced on mature plants during the summer.

This is a fairly popular species and is easy to grow in a half-depth pot. The slight bluish color to its body is an added bonus and it is not particularly cold sensitive.

Most Ferocactus have a small nectary in the upper part of the areole and this will, at certain times of the year, mainly in autumn, exude a sugary secretion.

These are large growing plants.

At that time, as the temperatures drop and humidity rises, sooty mold can grow on this secretion that rather disfigures the plant. Plants will benefit from spraying with water during the late summer to remove the secretion or spray the plants with a fungicide and allow the air to circulate around it. Stains can often be removed by spraying with warm soapy water and using a small brush.

Ferocactus pilosus

This plant has produced beautiful red spines on new growth.

This is a very distinctive plant at any size on account of its bright red spines. In the wild, it is an outstanding species, as it grows to about 10 feet (3m) tall and nearly 2 feet (60cm) in diameter. It also branches from the base to make large groups. These plants will flower during the summer when they reach about 9 inches (22cm) tall. The flowers are yellow to red and about 1.5 inches (4cm) in diameter.

It is also known under its synonym *F. stainesii,* which does not have the small wispy white radial spines. From the time it grows to about 4 inches (10cm) tall, it is impossible to confuse it with any other Ferocactus species.

Ferocactus pilosus seems to tolerate temperatures of about 42°F (5°C) and is easy to grow from seed. In frost-free areas, these make superb colorful plants, either as specimens or when planted as a colony.

Ferocactus wislizenii v. herrerae

These superb large-growing plants are a little more columnar than some, reaching up to 6 feet (2m) tall and 18 inches (45cm) in diameter, which is a little smaller than the species. Deep spiralling ribs support large, flattened, fish-hook-like spines and numerous pale star-like, radial spines.

The species *F. wislizenii* and *F. herrerae* are very closely related and there is some debate as to whether they are distinct enough to be separate species. Their flowers are similar although *F.wislizenii* can have a more yellowish flower than *F. herrerae,* which can have a red mid vein in its slightly more orangy flowers.

Both species are excellent examples of large-growing barrel cacti, which have fierce, fish-hook spines. Both are easy to grow from seed, but do not flower until they reach about 8 inches (20cm) in diameter. Regular repotting will encourage faster growth and flowering size can be reached in under ten years from seed.

The large spines of this plant make it distinctive.

Gymnocalycium bruchii

This charming, small-headed species offsets freely to make mutiple-headed clumps. Many, delicate, pale pink flowers are produced in spring from the crown of the plant.

Sometimes this plant is sold as a "blue-flowered" cactus. This misleading description originates from a printing error in a well-known cactus book that was published with a blue cast to a whole block of pictures.

An easy plant to grow from seed, it flowers at about 2–3 years old, when only about 1 inch (2.5cm) in diameter. It seems to prefer shade in the height of summer, as it can soon dry up. Its growing season seems to be from early spring until about mid-summer.

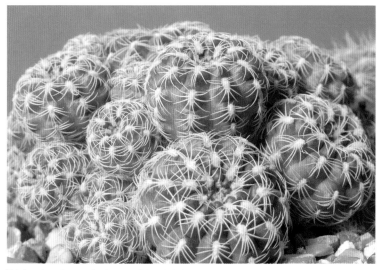

This is a charming species forms multi-headed clumps.

Gymnocalycium mihanovichii 'Hibotan'

Also known as 'Red Top' or 'Ruby Ball,' the strange form of this species has been developed over many years by grafting odd colored patches, which these plants often produce, until they are of a uniform red, purple, or black. This red form completely lacks any chlorophyll (the green substance of plants that transforms light into energy) and so must be grafted. It is often seen grafted on Hylocereus, on which it grows very well. Unfortunately Hylocereus is a very tropical species and needs a high winter temperature. In higher latitudes these plants can be very difficult to keep through the winter.

As these plants lack chlorophyll, they cannot exist on their own and must be grafted onto a

This unusual novelty plant is known as lollipop cactus.

green body or stock, which makes and supplies the necessary sustenance for the plant. For this reason they cannot be grafted onto a short stock and therefore always look a little like a lollipop. They are probably more popular with the general public as a plant novelty than with cactus collectors.

Gymnocalycium horstii

This distinctive species from Brazil makes large heads up to about 8 inches (20cm) tall and in diameter. It soon clusters mostly by short stolons to make large clumps. As it has only five to six very distinct ribs and few spines, it is unlike any other Gymnocalycium apart from *G. bueneckeri,* which used to be classified as a variety. It has a bright, light green, body color and its flowers are normally salmon pink and about 4 inches (10cm) in diameter. *G. bueneckeri* has a darker matt-green body and a pinker flower.

Both of these species prefer a winter temperature of about 50°F (10°C) to grow well. At lower temperatures, they are prone to losing their roots in winter and need to be re-rooted again in the spring.

This species is not difficult to grow from seed and usually there is a variation in the spination of plants from the same batch of seeds.

This species grows to be large, and forms clumps.

Gymnocalycium quehlianum

This plant has a short-growing, hemispherical body, which has the shape of a mushroom cap. Its gray-green to reddish-brown body will reach 4–6 inches (10–15cm) in diameter with great age. It is usually solitary but does occasionally offset. It has 11–14 low, rounded ribs separated by vertical furrows, and it has little chin-like tubercles. This species, and others that are very similar, are very distinctive and should be included in every collection. The beautiful 2 inch (5cm) diameter, white flowers have a red center that is visible when the flowers are fully open. Most Gymnocalyciums will not open their flowers fully in poor light or shade. The name Gymnocalycium means "a naked bud." In the case of *G. quehlianum,* these buds are a delightful shade of gray and appear as if they have been cast in metal.

Gymnocalycium quehlianum has a squat gray body.

These plants are easy to grow from seed and will flower when about 3 years old and just a little more than an inch (2.5cm) in diameter.

Gymnocalycium saglionis

Gymnocalycium saglionis grows into a large plant.

This is a large-growing Gymnocalyciums and is a very distinctive species. It will grow to about 6 inches (15cm) tall and 12 inches (30cm) or more in diameter. It has 1–3 straight central spines and up to about 12 curved spines that arch back toward the plant's body. A comparatively low number of ribs means that the plant has very pronounced large rounded tubercles. Short, squat, pinkish flowers are produced from the crown of this plant in summer. The flowers are very rich in numerous stamens and pollen.

The small reddish seed-pods, when ripe, will split vertically so that both the seeds and juice are "squirted" out. This species does best at the slightly higher temperature of 50°F (10°C) in winter, as otherwise it is prone to rotten patches that can kill the entire plant. Unlike some smaller species, it seems to revel in full sun during the summer.

Hatiora salicornioides

Hatiora is a small group of Brazilian cacti that now include the plants often referred to as Easter cactus.

Hatiora salicornioides is a strange small, bushy plant with very short cylindrical stems that swell toward their tips making them look like little bottles. This has led to the common name of drunkard's dream.

The plants are initially erect but with age the stems become arching and then pendent, branching from the tips. Small, yellow flowers are produced in spring and summer on well-cultivated plants.

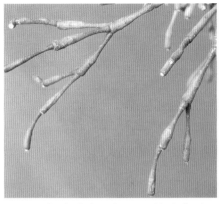

Drunkard's dream has unusual bottle-like stem sections.

This epiphyte likes a bright situation, but not full sun. It really needs a minimum winter temperature of 50°F (10°C) to grow well, although it will survive slightly lower temperatures.

These plants seem to prefer a rich well-drained compost. When grown in a bright situation, their dark green stems will take on a reddish hue. Plants that are too cold or lack food will become a yellowish green.

These plants are normally propagated from cuttings, which are best taken in spring. These should be allowed to callous and then potted in small pots and kept just damp and warm so that they root down fairly quickly. Put several cuttings in the same pot to make an "instant" new plant.

Lepismium bolivianum

The genera of Lepismium and Rhipsalis are very closely related. Many plants have at one time or another been included in both. Currently the distinction between the two is the way they branch. Rhipsalis is for plants that branch in whorls (several new stems produced together) from the tips of the stems. Lepismium is for plants that branch laterally (from the sides of stems). These epiphytic cacti mostly have angular stems, which are often spiny and produce small flowers during winter and spring, followed by attractive small berries.

Lepismium bolivianum has slender, flattened, pendent stems.

Lepismium bolivianum has narrow ribbon-like, flat stems that are initially erect but soon become arching and pendent. These stems can easily grow to 2 feet (60cm) or more in length during a season. The small flowers are orangey yellow and mainly produced in spring. It is an easy plant to grow and makes a very attractive subject for a hanging basket.

Lepismium ianthothele

This species was formerly included in Pfeiffera. It has narrow, erect, ribbed stems that have spiny areoles but its weak stems will soon become pendent. At first glance, it looks more like an Aporocactus. There are several forms of this species, which vary in spination, stem thickness, and size.

Its small, half-inch (1cm) diameter flowers are a pinkish white and are produced laterally along the stems in late spring. These are followed by small berries, which when ripe become translucent and resemble miniature gooseberries.

Like most of this Brazilian genus, it really needs a minimum of 50°F (10°C) in winter to grow well. It seems to prefer a bright situation and moderate amounts of water during the spring and summer. It makes an ideal subject for a hanging basket and is fairly distinctive in this group of plants.

The stems of *Lepismium ianthothele* soon become pendent.

Lepismium monacanthum

The bright orange flowers of this species make it quite distinctive. It has both three-angled and flattened stems and is up to about 1 inch (2.5cm) wide. Areoles along notched stems produce one or two fairly stout, short, light-colored spines. Like most plants of this genus, stems are initially erect and can grow to a foot (30cm) or more tall before becoming pendent. Flowers are produced in the spring but often more are produced during the summer months. This slightly larger growing species is good for hanging baskets and is one of the few species that has found its way into commercial horticulture. It likes a bright situation but when grown in full sun, its stems will soon wither to papery dry remnants.

One of the few species that has orange flowers.

Leuchtenbergia principis

This strange Agave-like cactus has long angular tubercles rather like leaves. The areoles at the ends of the tubercles produce long, papery, flat spines which can be up to 6 inches (15cm) long. In the wild, these plants can be difficult to find, as they can easily be mistaken for clumps of coarse grass.

They are thought to be very close-ly related to Ferocactus, with which they will hybridize. They produce large, bright, yellow flowers up to 3 inches (7.5cm) in diameter in spring and summer and will start to flower when quite small, usually 3–4 years old from seed. In higher latitudes, the plants seem to flower much better when grown in full sun.

This cactus looks similar to the Agave family.

They develop a very tuberous root system, which in great age become a small trunk. They are usually solitary, but old specimens will sometimes branch. They are not one of the easiest plants to grow. During the summer months they seem to need moderate amounts of water to grow well but their tuberous roots can rot if the plants are kept wet. It is probably best grown in a very free-draining compost and watered more frequently. Plants should be kept dry in winter.

Mammillaria

Of all the genera of cacti grown in higher latitudes, this must be the most popular. They are mostly small-growing plants that flower well; this makes them ideal to grow indoors or in a glasshouse where space is always at a premium.

Mammillaria is an easy group of plants to grow, although there are a few which are more challenging. They need well-drained compost in containers 3–4 inches (7.5–10cm) deep. During the spring and summer, they should be watered well and then allowed to dry before watering again. With large containers, give sufficient water so that they will dry out in about 10 days. Plants should be fed regularly during the summer to encourage flowering the following year.

Mammillaria bocasana

An easy Mammillaria to grow, this one produces cream to pink flowers continuously throughout the summer.

For many cactus collectors this is often one of the first cactus that they acquire. It makes a domed hemispherical plant body, which soon offsets to create a mound. It is densely covered with long, hair-like, white spines that conceal small, hooked central spines. The plants have a slightly tuberous root, which can make them a little

The more densely spined form *multilanata*.

susceptible to rotting if kept in wet soil; otherwise they are easy to grow.

These plants normally produce a cream flower, but some can be a bit yellow while others are delicate shades of pink. Some plants can become a little more columnar than others and offset less frequently. The spination is very variable and the plant shown on the opposite page (*f. multilanata*) is a more densely spined form. These plants are easy to grow and will soon make large plants. A 10 inch (25cm) pan of these in flower for most of the summer is something that most collectors will enjoy and can be proud of. As an added bonus, in the autumn the plants will produce their seed pods, which are like long, slender, bright red worms. The number will depend on how many flowers have been pollinated. This is a must for every collection.

Mammillaria bombycina

In earlier days, a well-grown plant of this species would always do very well in botanical shows, as larger specimens are outstandingly beautiful.

Some forms grow into hemispherical mounds, while others have multiple stems. The flowers form a ring at the crown.

There are many different forms of this species. Some plants grow into beautiful hemispherical mounds, with one main head and numerous smaller ones surrounding it. Some plants produce heads that are much more finger-like and make clumps of short columnar heads.

The spination is also variable. The hooked central spine can be red, yellow, or brownish, which makes each plant an individual. They are all worth growing and with time make the most beautiful clumps.

They are not difficult plants to grow, but prefer a free-draining compost as they are prone to rotting if kept wet all the time. These are easy to grow from seed and should flower when about 3–4 years old.

Mammillaria candida

This species needs extra calcium in the soil.

The dense short white spines on this species make it almost impossible to see the plant body beneath them. These plants are comparatively small-growing; a large plant is perhaps only 4–5 inches (10–12cm) in diameter and about 6 inches (15cm) tall.

It is a little more of a challenge to grow than some, as it can be prone to losing its roots. It is one of those species that will do very much better if chalk is added to its compost.

Plants will flower when about 2–3 inches (5–7.5cm) in diameter and will produce creamy pinkish-brown flowers in spring and summer. If these are pollinated, then short, fat, orangey seedpods will just protrude through the dense spines in the autumn.

Propagation is normally from seed. Care should be taken with larger seedlings to make sure they do not sit in wet compost for long, as they are prone to rotting.

Mammillaria carmenae

This is one of the newer Mammillarias to come into cultivation. It is a small-growing, clumping species, which has a dense covering of short spines. The spine color is normally a yellowish brown, but this is quite variable, ranging from very pale yellow to an almost reddish brown.

These plants flower freely during the summer months, producing a variety of flower colors, ranging from white to various shades of pale pink.

It does not seem particularly difficult to grow, although it seems to prefer a winter temperature of 50°F (10°C). It also likes a well-drained

This plant has a very variable spine and flower color.

compost, as it can be a little prone to rotting if wet for too long.

Large clumps of this species are magnificent. However, these take some years to grow, perhaps 20 years from seed.

Mammillaria chionocephala

An old trailing plant.

This fairly slow-growing species will eventually grow to about 10 inches (25cm) tall and around 4–5 inches (10–12cm) in diameter. It is a very neat plant with short spines and produces large amounts of white wool around the growing point, giving the impression of a very fluffy plant. The rings of cream to pink flowers are produced at regular intervals during the spring and summer.

These plants are at their best when 3–4 inches (7.5–10cm) in diameter. As the plants age, they become taller and eventually prostrate, which can be a problem for pot-grown specimens. Every plant is slightly different and several will enhance any larger collection. They are easy to grow from seed and will reach flowering size in about 3 years.

Mammillaria elongata

The small, finger-like stems of this clumping plant are densely covered in short, radiating spines. Small, yellow flowers are produced from its upper stems in the spring and summer.

An easy species to grow, it is popular with collectors. Its short spines vary in color from pale yellow, through dark yellow, to brownish and red-brown. This makes it possible to collect perhaps up to 50 different forms of this species, all of which look different. There are also a few plants around with pink flowers.

Occasionally, in an old plant, the main stem may either dry up or rot off and the rest of the plant will start to look dehydrated. In such a case the plant can easily be pulled apart and its cuttings will root down easily. In fact, often many of its heads will already have a root system.

This species is usually propagated from cuttings of the less common spine color forms, or from seed. Seedlings should flower when 2–3 years old.

Mammillaria elongata has finger-like golden spines.

Mammillaria geminispina

This large, clump-forming species makes magnificent specimen plants, densely covered in glassy white, almost shining spines. The areoles produce dense, short, white, radial spines and 2–6 long, white, central spines that are often curved. There are many forms of this species, which have slightly different spination and spine lengths, but all are beautiful plants. Probably the nicest are those with the longest central spines. Very small carmine flowers are produced in spring and autumn. These are followed by small carmine-red seedpods. It is not at all unusual for the pods to split open and for their color to stain the surrounding spines. This color soon bleaches or washes out. This is not one of the most floriferous species but it is collected for its general appearance.

Mammillaria geminispina is a beautiful long-spined clumping plant.

One of the prettiest, larger, clump-forming Mammillarias, this should be in every collection. This species is normally grown from seed, but be aware that some variation is normally to be seen between individual seedlings.

Mammillaria hahniana

A species that has been around in cultivation for a very long time and is justifiably still a very popular plant. The compact, globular body is usually solitary and covered in long, wispy, white, hair-like spines. In the spring, the plants produce rings of deep carmine flowers around the crown, a beautiful contrast to the dense, white, woolly covering.

The long, hair-like spines have given it the common name of old lady cactus. In the autumn, these plants produce small, erect, carmine seedpods rather like a ring of candles. This has given rise to its other common name of birthday cake.

These plants  are usually grown from seed and normally there is a great variation in the spine length between different plants. Seedlings will normally flower when quite small at 2–3 years old from seed. Eventually the plants will grow to about 5 inches (12cm) in diameter and perhaps 9–10 inches (22–25cm) tall.

This is another must for every collection. It is easy to grow and flower and beautiful to look at.

Mammillaria hahniana has very variable spine lengths.

Mammillaria magnimamma

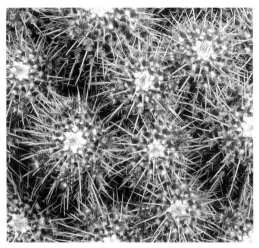

The plant bodies are generally spherical in shape but can be extremely variable.

Mammillaria magnimamma is now the correct name for a whole range of species that were at one time considered different. This means that this species is now quite variable. The plant bodies are generally hemispherical in shape, occasionally becoming short and columnar, and usually offsetting freely to make large clumps. Plants have large, long, often angular tubercles. Like many Mammillarias, these have a divided areole, the flowers and tufts of white wool being produced at the base of the tubercle on the body of the plant. The tubercles usually have few spines, which can be small or large, short or long. In most plants, the dark green plant body is easy to see, and hardly masked by the spines.

Rings of flowers are produced in the spring. These vary from cream to pink to carmine, and often have a deeper mid vein.

These are extremely robust plants, they will survive abuse from the non-collector and still thrive. Eventually, these plants will make very large clumps. Although this is a very variable species, they are usually consistent from seed, so seedlings from the same plant will be fairly uniform.

Mammillaria mazatlanensis

This is one of a group of Mammillarias, which, although small-growing, has unusually large flowers that are produced much later in the year, during early summer. More temperamental to grow than others of the Mammillaria genus, it is prone to rotting if kept too wet or watered too early or late in the year.

A small-clumping species with finger-like stems, it makes clumps up to about 6 inches (15cm) in diameter. Cerise flowers are produced over a certain period from the upper part of the stems in early summer. These flowers grow to about an inch (2.5cm) in diameter, which seems large for a relatively small plant.

Although these plants are not difficult to grow for the average collector, they can be challenging for the novice. Plants are usually propagated from seed and should flower in 2–3 years when they are still quite small.

Mammillaria mazatlanensis
is later flowering than many species.

Mammillaria plumosa

A well-grown specimen of this species always used to win in a cactus show until quite recently. It makes a beautiful domed mound, densely covered in interlocking white feathery spines. It looks something like a fluffy cauliflower.

Although the individual heads of this plant are only 2–4 inches (5–10cm) in diameter, it offsets quite freely to make a large clump. It makes several different growth forms from golf ball-like individual heads to those that make a smooth mound. Creamy white flowers are produced from mid winter until early spring and in warm weather are sweetly scented.

It is not one of the easiest plants to grow, as it can be prone to rotting if kept wet and desiccate if kept too dry for long periods. One of the problems is that it naturally grows on rocks and never really makes an extensive root system. The addition of calcium (ground chalk) to compost will help to make a better root system. During the summer it should be watered slightly less than normal cactus. During the autumn and winter, it should not be allowed to dry completely for long periods as this can lead to dehydration. If grown in a pot or pan then an occasional light bottom watering will be beneficial.

If the plant does either begin to rot, or individual heads dry out, these can be removed quite easily. If the main plant begins to suffer, then the individual heads can be separated and rerooted in the spring.

Mammillaria plumosa resembles a cauliflower.

Mammillaria poselgeri

There are a small group of Mammillarias that have a zygomorphic (lopsided) flower. These used to be included in the genus Cochemiea, but are now considered by many to be Mammillarias.

This species has cylindrical stems that are initially erect but later become trailing, growing to a foot (30cm) or more in length. It offsets slowly from the base to make clumps. On young plants, the upper part of the areole can clearly be seen as a little dot between their tubercles.

These are unusual shaped flowers for a Mammillaria.

As the plant ages and matures, these eventually begin to produce woolly tufts. This is an indication that the plant has reached flowering size, usually 5–7 years from seed. Bright cerise flowers are produced by mature plants in spring, summer, and autumn.

They should be grown in a sunny position. Their light green stems will take on a reddish hue. This is not a difficult plant to grow but is still relatively rare in cultivation, due to its comparatively slow rate of growth to maturity.

Mammillaria rhodantha

Although initially globular, these plants soon become columnar. As they age and grow taller, they become prostrate. This species usually branches from the top. The growing point divides (dichotomous branching) and gradually becomes two heads. This is repeated many times on old plants. Occasionally, such plants will branch conventionally from the base.

This is a very variable species with several varieties. Individual plants always have a very neat appearance with their curved spines regularly arranged. These spines can be red to pale yellow at the extremes and all shades in between. The length is also very variable, giving many similar yet different looking plants.

These are easy to grow from seed and should flower when 2–3 years old.

This plant is the golden-spined form.

Mammillaria sempervivi

A small-growing species, its bluish green heads grow up to about 4 inches (10cm) in diameter and are normally solitary. The tubercles have short spines rather like stars, usually dark brown to black in color. Old plants produce quite large amounts of wool from their areoles, and on a plant that is not watered overhead, this can gradually build up until it rather resembles a powder puff.

This is not a difficult plant to grow and will flower when only 2–3 years old from seed and about 2 inches (5cm) in diameter.

The body of *Mammillaria sempervivi* is small and has long tubercles and short spines.

Mammillaria sheldonii

The more densely clumping form *gueldemanniana*.

A number of similar species have now been aggregated under the name of *Mammillaria sheldonii*. These plants are summer-flowering and mostly have larger than normal cerise flowers. They seem to start growing 2–3 weeks later in the year than the other Mammillarias and are also susceptible to low temperatures; a minimum of 50°F (10°C) is recommended.

Although these plants are more challenging to grow, they flower at a time of year when there are not so many flowers and these are bright and cheerful. They are well worth including in any comprehensive collection. The form *gueldemanniana* has slightly narrower heads and forms clumps more quickly than the species. Propagation is normally from seed, as cuttings can be very slow to root.

Mammillaria spinosissima v. pilcayensis

Mammillaria spinosissima is a medium-sized plant with cylindrical heads, which will eventually grow to about 20 inches (50cm) tall and up to 4 inches (10cm) in diameter. These plants are attractive with a moderately dense spine covering in various shades of white to yellow-brown. Their straight central spine(s) are often brightly colored, often red, and a good contrast to the radial spines.

During the spring, and often again in summer or autumn, their plants will produce rings of bright pink flowers around the upper part of the stem. Plants are normally solitary. As the stems grow taller they tend to arch towards the sun.

The variety *pilcayensis* has spines that are all mostly the same length and provide an evenly dense covering. They are often lighter in color with just a hint of color in the central spines. It is a species that always looks very neat and tidy.

All forms of *Mammillaria spinosissima* are worth growing, even if just for the flowers. They are easy to raise from seed and there is normally variety in the seedlings. They should flower when 3–4 years old from seed.

This plant has more densely packed spines than the species.

Mammillaria vetula ssp. gracilis

This species is almost impossible to repot without falling apart.

These plants are much better known under their old name of *Mammillaria gracilis* or *M. fragilis*. This is a very small-headed and clumping species, the heads little bigger than peas, and making large clumps. The problem with them is that the heads are very lightly attached to the main stems and any jolt to the plant or pot is likely to make the plant shed many of them. The plants produce small creamy white flowers, mainly in the spring.

This is a real beginner's plant, easy to grow despite whatever you do to it. It is easy to propagate by detaching an offset, which will root readily, if placed on any damp surface.

The real problem is how to repot a plant without it all breaking up. There is no secret to this apart from being very careful. The best advice is to plant several small plants or offsets in an 8–10 inch (20–25cm) pan, or whatever size you ultimately want, and to just be patient. It grows fairly quickly and, after a couple of years, you will have a beautiful plant without having to keep on potting it up. A well-grown plant is brilliant white, and the body almost invisible beneath the small dense spines.

Mammillaria zeilmanniana

Of all the cacti, this must be the one that sells the most. Millions are grown every year and sold as flowering houseplants. This small-headed species clumps easily to make specimen plants up to about 10 inches (25cm) in diameter. Once it reaches this size, it seems quite prone to rotting. However, perhaps it is just old age and this is a short-lived plant.

The normal form has reddish hooked central spines and a bright cerise flower. There is some variation in the spination, and flowers can be anything from white to pink or a deep cerise. A well-grown clump, covered in rings of flowers in the spring, is enough to encourage many to start collecting cactus plants.

It is an easy plant to grow from seed and sometimes will flower when less than a year old and little bigger than a pea. No

collection or windowsill is complete without at least one example of this species.

One of the most popular of all the cacti.

Matucana aureiflora

Like many of the old Submatucana, the globular Matucanas, they were transferred to Borzicactus. As this genus has now been split up again, these have now been transferred to Matucana.

Matucana aureiflora is the most distinctive of this group as its plant body is a depressed globular shape, bright green with short, yellow spines. The flowers it produces are also unique as they are bright yellow and open fully. The flowers are produced in spring from the crown of the plant. If the plant is cross-pollinated and seed pods develop, these are small and green when ripe and split from top to bottom, releasing

This cactus flowers easily in spring.

the seeds. This is probably one of the easiest of the Matucanas to grow and is tolerant of slightly lower winter temperatures, probably as low as about 44°F (6°C). It is also easy to grow from seed and should flower at about 3–4 years old when it is about 2 inches (5cm) in diameter.

Matucana madisoniorum

This is a globular blue-bodied plant that is almost spineless. When it is growing during the summer, the new growth will produce quite long, slender black spines but these are normally shed after a season or less.

Like most of this group, it has tubular flowers that open at the tip. These plants are pollinated by humming birds, which is unusual for globular plants. Flowers are produced in batches from spring to autumn and are a bright red in color.

The Matucanas are native to Peru and are not tolerant of low temperatures. They need a minimum of 50°F (10°C) during winter. In summer, they should be grown in full sun.

These are not difficult plants to grow from seed, but should be kept warm. Plants will flower at about 2 inches (5cm) diameter when 3–4 years old.

Bright red flowers are produced from time to time during the summer.

Matucana paucicostatus

This small-growing species is similar to the previous species except that it is much smaller, offsets freely, and has short, flexible, twisted spines. It has 7–11 ribs which are divided up into conical tubercles. Tubular, bright red flowers sprout

erect from the crown of the plant and are zygo-morphic (lopsided), pointing their faces out sideways. This species is not tolerant of low temperatures and requires a minimum of 50°F (10°C). Plants of this type should be kept dry in winter.

It is not difficult to grow from seed but should be kept warm. Plants flower in 2–3 years from seed.

This cactus usually produces clusters of flowers at a time.

Opuntia microdasys

One of the largest groups of cactus—and one that also has the widest distribution from Canada to Chile and Argentina—are the prickly pears, the genus Opuntia. They are an extremely diverse group which range from large tree-like specimens, to bushes and alpine ground cover plants.

Opuntia microdasys is a small-growing bush species from Mexico and there are many different forms of it in cultivation. These have different colored glochids, the very short tufted spines, which are in abundance in each areole. These range from white to cream through yellow to reddish brown. The small pads are flattened stems and these are usually round to ovoid in shape.

This is a very popular species in cultivation and, when well grown, always looks attractive. The disadvantage is that its glochids are very lightly attached and are easily dislodged. It is a plant that is best handled with gloves to avoid getting them into the skin. These are not poisonous but irritating for a little while. It is not tolerant of low temperatures and needs a minimum temperature of 50°F (10°C).

This cactus is always popular as a house plant.

Opuntia robusta

Opuntia robusta has large pale blue pads.

This is a large-growing, tree-like species. It can make numerous stems that grow to about 10 feet (3m) tall. Its large, bluish pads are often spherical or slightly elliptical. Two-inch (5cm) yellow flowers are produced on larger specimens in summer, when they reach about 4 feet (1.2m) tall. The pads on this species are often likened to blue dinner plates. Sometimes they have no spines or only one to two stout white spines. It is a quick growing and robust species, reputed to be fairly hardy. In higher latitudes in glasshouses, it seems prone to rot at temperatures below 45°F (7°C).

It is normally propagated from cuttings but does grow quite easily from seed. Some Opuntia seeds can take several years to germinate, but this species seems relatively quick to do so.

Opuntia santa rita

This bushy, round, padded species will eventually grow to about 6 feet (2m) tall. Each pad grows to about 6–8 inches (15–20cm) in diameter and has brown glochids. Its bluish pads turn red and then violet in the sunshine. In a glasshouse in higher latitudes, they will show some color but not the bright violet of outdoor cultivation. These plants are often spineless but some pads do often make a few long black spines from the upper part of each pad.

It is a species that will flower when fairly small and has beautiful yellow flowers with deep red centers.

A prickly pear with bright yellow and red flowers.

When grown in a pot, it can easily be kept to a neat and manageable shape.

It is a fairly easy plant to cultivate but, unless it gets very dehydrated, needs a minimum temperature of 45°F (7°C) in winter. When it is propagated from cuttings, it will root easily.

Opuntia scheerii

This attractive Opuntia is sprawling in habit and grows to about 3 feet (1m) tall. Its oblong to round pads normally grow to 6–9 inches (15–22cm) long. This plant has golden glochids with 10–12 short, needle-like spines. The plants also produce long, golden to white hair, which in some specimens can almost cover the stems. This makes a very attractive plant as it grows larger, giving the impression of a "golden" prickly pear. Spines are very lightly attached to the plant, so it needs to be placed where it will not get brushed against. Well worth cultivating in any medium-sized collection, this species is normally propagated from cuttings in summer which will root easily.

These pads are densely covered in hair-like spines.

Opuntia subulata monstrose

This is an example of the cylindrical, stemmed Opuntias. The genus Opuntia was in the past comprised of many individual groups of plants, which were all united under Opuntia. Currently, several botanists now believe that the different groups should be separated from the main genus.

Opuntia subulata is a tall-growing bush or tree with long cylindrical stems. Its tubercles are sparsely arranged around its stems. Like most of this group of Opuntias, it produces short cylindrical leaves on new growth at the tips of the stems. These are usually kept until a period of drought or dormancy, when they are nearly all shed.

The long spines are fairly sparse, but very sharp and barbed, so that care is needed when handling this plant. The monstrose form shown here makes fairly compact plants with short and deformed branching stems. It is cultivated as a novelty plant.

The smaller growing and clumping monstrose form.

Opuntia verschafeltii

A small-growing, bushy and slender-stemmed cylindrical species, the form normally cultivated has stems little thicker than a pencil and often completely spineless. These stems are mostly short, up to 4–5 inches (10–12cm) long, or very

Opuntia verschafeltii has slender almost spineless stems.

short, like little balls. Larger specimens will flower quite profusely, producing red flowers at the tips of the stems.

After several years of cultivation this plant can become very untidy and it is best to root some cuttings from it and start a new plant. This species seems quite tolerant of low temperatures if dry, but during the summer months seems to need more water than many other cacti.

An interesting little plant to grow, it is quite rewarding if you manage to grow a specimen-sized plant that will flower well.

Oreocereus celsianus

These plants are widespread in the wild and in most habitats vary greatly in size and spination. As they are very variable, many names in the past have been attributed for local forms of the plant.

These plants are tall column cactus that reach up to about 6 feet (2m) tall and 3–4 inches (7.5–10cm) in diameter, and branch from the base. They are usually densely covered in long, white, hair-like spines and have a few stout long spines from each areole. The common name for these plants is old man of the Andes. Extremely variable, some have little wool, some are shorter growing, some have red central spines, some yellow, and in some they are absent.

These are slow-growing plants and take many, many years to reach their flowering size of 3–4 feet (1–1.2m) tall.

The common name for *Oreocereus celsianus* is the old man of the Andes.

They should be grown in well-drained compost as, like most slow-growing plants, they can be susceptible to rot if kept in wet compost.

A minimum temperature of about 50°F (10°C) is ideal for them, as at lower temperatures the plants can rot. This usually attacks the growing point and on larger plants will just kill the tops of the stems. Plants are also prone to marking badly at low temperatures.

Oreocereus doelzianus f. sericata

Oreocereus doelzianus was previously included in Morawtzia. These are much smaller growing Oreocereus. They are bushy, branching from the base, with stems up to 3 feet (1m) tall but only 2–3 inches (5–7.5cm) in diameter. The stems are slightly woolly and fairly spiny with golden to red spines. When the plants reach flowering size, the crown of the 2–3 feet (60–100cm) tall stems swell and produce long wool and tubular red to carmine flowers that open out at the tips. The cephalium is terminal and, although it will continue to produce flowers, it will not make any further growth.

The form *sericata* is a smaller-growing plant with stems 1–2 feet (30–60cm) tall and densely covered in long white, hair-like spines, like cotton wool. As in the species the stems produce dense white wool at their tips when they reach flowering size. The flowers are various shades of red.

These plants branch freely and soon make clumps. The old flowering stems eventually become untidy and marked and are best removed from time to time. These can be used as cuttings. Although plants are reasonably robust, seedlings seem to be a little more susceptible to lower temperatures and are probably best kept at a minimum of 50°F (10°C) for the first 2–3 years.

The short, densely hairy stems flower easily at the tip.

Oreocereus trollii

This species is similar to *Oreocereus celsianus* but is much shorter growing. From observing damaged plants in the wild, it appears that this species has a very narrow vascular bundle, while *O. celsianus* has a wide one. Because of this narrow vascular bundle, the plants are not able to support a tall stem.

This species branches from the base and the stems of wild plants are no taller than knee height, about 2 feet (60cm). The stems are thick and chunky and up to about 5 inches (12cm) in diameter. As they continue to grow, they will become prostrate, turning up at the tips. In cultivation in glasshouses, without all the rigors of the weather and a more frequent supply of water, the stems will grow a little taller. The plant bodies are usually densely covered in long, twisted, white, hair-like spines that wrap themselves around the stem. Through this grow many stout central spines, often reddish in color.

These beautiful plants are not difficult to grow but are very slow, like *O. celsiasus*, and require a similar treatment. Plants are normally propagated from seed.

This plant is a very old specimen that demonstrates it is slow-growing.

Pachycereus gatesii

This comparatively small-growing Pachycereus only grows to about 6 feet (2m) tall. It is a bushy plant with many stems, both from the base and branching from higher up. When its stems reach flowering size, about 4 feet (1.2m), then they start to produce extra long and softer spines (pseudocephalium). The small one inch (2.5cm) diameter pink flowers are produced at night from this zone and fade in the morning. Flowering-size plants are usually quite prolific in the number of flowers they produce. It does not appear to be self-fertile, but the seedpods are small, less than an inch (2.5cm) in diameter.

It is not a difficult plant to grow, but it is still quite rare in cultivation. It can be grown from cuttings that seem very slow to root, as they take up to a year or more. It is not difficult to grow from seed, if any is available.

This clumping plant produces extra spines at the top of stems that are ready for flowering.

Pachycereus pringlei

This giant tree-like cactus is a native of the Sonoran desert and the area south of it into Mexico. It will grow to nearly 40 feet (12m) tall and has a trunk about 2 feet (60cm) in diameter. The plants are only lightly spined with short spines up to about an inch (2.5cm) in diameter. Unlike many of the Pachycereus, the flowers are open both day and night on large and mature specimens.

This outstanding feature plant of the desert bears little resemblance to small seedlings usually seen in collections. It is not a difficult plant to grow and after its first 3–4 years is not particularly slow, although it will take many decades to grow to maturity. Seedlings are probably best given a minimum temperature of 50°F (10°C) during winter.

This cactus is slow-growing, but eventually becomes quite large.

Parodia chrysacanthion

This beautiful small-growing Parodia has a flattened, globular body that grows to about 4–5 inches (10–12cm) tall and about 10 inches (25cm) in diameter. It is densely covered in long, soft, golden spines, creating the effect of a golden ball. In age, the oldest spines can discolor to brownish-yellow. When this plant is

This is one of the easier Parodias to grow.

growing well, its crown is densely covered in short, white, tufted, hair-like spines and it is from these that the nearly one inch (2.5cm) wide golden flowers appear in summer. It is not a particularly difficult plant to grow but like most of the old Parodias it really needs a minimum temperature of about 50°F (10°C) in winter.

This group of plants seems to lose its roots very easily if kept dry for long periods during winter. As they need the occasional light watering during this time, they need to be kept warmer. These plants should be checked in spring to make sure they are firm in their pots and have a good root system, as otherwise a rootless plant sitting in damp compost is likely to rot. Very old plants will grow to quite a large size, but most will die before they grow to more than about 5 inches (13cm) in diameter.

Propagate them from seed. Seedlings may take some while to germinate and then they stay very small for a long time. When they start growing, they usually catch up with other plants after a couple of years.

Parodia erubescens

In recent times, many new species have been discovered in Notocactus and Parodia and these have now been shown to be so closely related that they have been amalgamated. This species is much better known under its old name of *Notocactus schlosseri*.

This is a small-growing, globular plant, which eventually becomes cylindrical and then prostrate up to about 9 inches (23cm) long. It has a dense covering of short

The plant produces typically bright golden flowers.

white and red spines and produces 2 inch (5cm) diameter golden flowers during the spring and summer.

It is easy to grow from seed and flowers at about 2–3 years old when little more than an inch (2.5cm) in diameter. Older plants seem to be particularly prone to losing their roots, and these seem reluctant to regrow. It will probably grow much better if kept warmer in winter and given the occasional light watering when weather permits.

Parodia haselbergii v. graesneri

These two old species of Notocactus were among the link plants that have led to the two genera being amalgamated.

This is not one of the easiest plants to grow but is well worth the effort.

These are small-growing plants with depressed globular bodies. *P. haselbergii* has white spines and red flowers, while *v. graesneri* has golden spines and greenish flowers.

These are not very easy plants to grow and need a warm winter temperature with occasional water or their roots will die in long periods of drought. Grown well, these plants flower very early in the year, and are among the first of the globular types of cactus to flower each year.

These plants are normally propagated from seed and will flower at about 3–4 years old.

Parodia leninghausii

This species is much better known as *Notocactus leninghausii* or *Eriocactus leninghausii*. It is probably closer to Parodia than it is to Notocactus.

These plants are tall-growing, and reach to about 3 feet (1m) in height and about 3 inches (7.5cm) in diameter. They offset prolifically from their bases to make large clumps. Their main stems are quite soft in structure and will stay erect up to about I foot (30cm) high. A well-grown plant with lots of offsets may stay erect up to 2 feet (60cm) high, but beyond this its stems tend to become prostrate and turn up at the ends. This species is easy to grow from seed but germinated seeds take a long time before they really start to grow and then do so quite rapidly. Seedlings will flower when about 3–4 inches (7.5–10cm)

This cactus eventually grows quite tall and offsets freely.

tall. These plants grow much better in full sun and will produce a tighter body and brilliant golden spines under these conditions. Old plants will flower several times during the summer, and will produce numerous blooms that make a large head of flowers. These are pale yellow and about 2 inches (5cm) in diameter.

Parodia magnifica

This name is well justified by this species. There are two different forms of this plant in cultivation; one has fewer ribs than the other and offsets far less freely. Their bodies are blue-green and their ribs are fringed with white, radial spines and soft, golden, central spines. Bright, golden flowers are produced during the summer.

This is an easy species to grow, but it really needs a minimum winter temperature of about 50°F (10°C) for it to grow well. It will flower at about 3–4 years from seed. Growth is certainly not slow and clumping plants will probably need repotting at least once each year. As the plants grow larger, they become more beautiful and in time create clumps that easily reach 3 feet (1m) in diameter.

These beautiful blue-stemmed plants eventually make large clumps and produce bright yellow flowers.

Parodia microsperma

This Parodia now embodies many of the old Parodia species and has numerous synonyms.

The plant bodies are usually solitary but occasionally branch to make small clumps. They are globular to short cylindrical and usually have spiralling ribs. There are numerous radial spines and often up to four central spines which are sometimes hooked. The 1–2 inch (2.5–5cm) diameter flowers can be yellow through orange to red.

Like most of the old Parodias, they are not the easiest plants to grow. The main problem is that they loose their roots in the winter due to long periods of drought. In order to be able to give them occasional light waterings during winter, the plants must be kept warmer, a minimum of 50°F (10°C).

After germination from seed, Parodias seem to do nothing, and stay very small for a long time. When they start to grow, they grow rapidly and after a couple of years are the same size as other species.

Parodia microsperma is a slow-growing species.

Parodia ottonis

The small-growing Notocactus now embodies most of the similar looking species. Plants are flattened, globose, usually a pale green in color with few ribs and few spines. Often a few of these are up to about an inch (2.5cm) long, soft and dark in color. These plants normally make clumps by producing short underground stolons. These can easily be detached and often have their own independent root system.

This species has been around in cultivation for a very long time and is very robust and tolerant of neglect and lower temperatures if dry. The large 2 inch (5cm) diameter flowers are produced through the summer months.

It can be propagated from seed or by division.

Parodia ottonis is a small-growing, old favorite of cacti growers.

Parodia schumannianus v. claviceps

Parodia schumannianus v. claviceps is better known as *Notocactus claviceps*. The species *Parodia schumannianus* is a large one, growing up to 5 feet (1.5m) long and a foot (30cm) in diameter. It is sparsely spined with a woolly crown and produces 2 inch (5cm) diameter flowers in summer.

P. schumannianus v. claviceps is smaller than the species, but still a large plant. It is globular to short, cylindrical and up to about 2 feet (60cm) tall and nearly a foot in diameter. It may off-set from anywhere on its body to make large clumps. Its spination is soft and golden and fairly dense, although it does not obscure the plant body. Large, 2 inch (5cm) diameter, pale yellow flowers are produced at intervals during the summer.

This cactus produces a large squat body.

This is a beautiful plant to grow, as it is large and impressive and appears golden in color. It is easy to grow from seed, but really needs a minimum winter temperature of 50°F (10°C), at least when small. It is prone to rotting if kept in cold, damp compost for long periods.

Parodia tabularis

Formerly known as *Notocactus tabularis* or *N. concinnus v. tabularis*, this small-growing, depressed, globular to short cylindrical plant grows to about 3 inches (7.5cm) in diameter. It produces bright yellow, 2 inch (5cm) diameter flowers during the spring and summer months.

This is one of a small group of similar-looking Notocactus, whose identity has always caused some confusion. Most of the other similar species are now included in *Parodia concinna*.

These are easy plants to raise from seed but can be prone to loosing their roots during long periods of drought.

Parodia tabularis produces large bright flowers in summer.

Parodia tenuicylindrica

This diminuitive species grows to about 3 inches (7.5cm) tall and up to an inch (2.5cm) in diameter. Sometimes it branches from the base or in some forms it branches from short underground stolons. The yellow flowers are about 1 inch (2.5cm) in diameter.

This is a slow-growing species that needs very little room. There are no particular problems involved with growing this plant.

Parodia tenuicylindrica is a very small growing species.

Rebutia

This is another genus that has recently undergone a massive change. There used to be about 550 "species" of Rebutia. There were also about 180 "species" of Sulcorebutia and 30 or so "species" of Weingartia. These genera have all been amalgamated and there are now just over 50 accepted species. As will be obvious from this dramatic reduction in taxa, most species are quite variable. Most Rebutias are able to tolerate low temperatures if kept dry.

Rebutia arenacea

This old Sulcorebutia is now one of the two remaining species of predominantly yellow-flowered plants.

These are small-growing plants, mostly offsetting, some forms more prolifically than others. Plant bodies are 1–2 inches (2.5–5cm) in diameter and about the same in height. The normally bright yellow flowers are produced from the elon-

gated areoles on the sides of the plants in spring. Like many of the old Sulcorebutias, this species has a tuberous root. It is comparatively slow-growing and a large plant is perhaps contained in a 4 inch (10cm) pot. This makes the plants a little more difficult to grow than some other types of cacti. Most of the old Sulcorebutias will make much larger and more floriferous plants if grafted.

This is a very attractive species even when not in flower.

Rebutia canigueralii

A large number of the old Sulcorebutias are now included here. These are mostly small-growing and clumping species. Most have depressed, globular bodies and produce a mound of heads. In most, the spiralled ribs are distinctly tuberculate. Flower color is also very variable from the traditional red with a yellow throat to red, cerise, and purple. Although this is now a very varied species, if all the different forms are compared there are great similarities between them. Those that do not fit are proba-bly wrongly

This species is extremely variable.

named. In the past, this genus was so frag-mented with a multitude of different names that few people could identify plants with any degree of certainty.

These plants are not difficult to grow, but are slow and small. A large old plant would fit in a 4 inch (10cm) pot.

The three forms of f. rauschii.

Rebutia marsoneri

In its old sense, this was a yellow-flowered Rebutia, a small, depressed globular plant that offset freely to make clumps of heads up to 3 inches (7.5cm) in diameter and produced red buds and large 2 inch (5cm), rich golden flowers.

In recent times, a red flowered form was found. It has now been amalgamated with other species like *R. krainziana*, which had bright red flowers and a very distinctive globular body with bright white areoles, and very short bristle-like spines. So like most species in this group it is now quite variable.

It is easy to grow from seed and should flower when about 2 years old. A large plant will grow to about 10 inches (25cm) in diameter.

One of the few old yellow-flowered Rebutias.

Rebutia minuscula

Most of the very old traditional Rebutia species are now included under this classification. They were plants with short, depressed, globular bodies, dark green in color, which offset freely and produced flowers from the base of the plant in spring. Many had a poor and weak spination so that the body was clearly visible but some (like the old *R. senilis*) had a good covering of longer white spines. The flowers, 1–2 inches (2.5–5cm) in diameter,

f. violaciflora.

were mostly shades of orangey-red, red, and violet.

Having seen large collections of wild plants with their habitat data, no two plants appear to be identical as to flower color, petal shape, or body shape. They are all so closely related that it makes a lot of sense to amalgamate them in one botanical species. Probably some of the old names are worthy of being maintained either at form or cultivar level.

These are very easy plants to grow from seed and many will flower when about a year old and little more than pea size.

f. kesselringiana.

Rebutia narvaecensis

This charming little Rebutia is often erroneously seen as *R. espinosae*.

It is a small-growing plant that clusters freely to make clumps. Its dark green body produces numerous prominent, long white spines. The flowers are pro-

This plant is small and produces delicate pink flowers.

duced from the sides of the plants in spring and summer. Their delicate pale pink color makes this a very distinctive species. When it is growing well, it produces so many flowers that they completely cover the plant body.

This is still fairly uncommon in cultivation and seed is not often available. It is often propagated by rooting some of the offsets. When seed is available it is not difficult to grow and will flower at about 2–3 years old.

Rebutia neocummingii

This name now applies to most of the old genus Weingartia, with the exception of a few very distinct species.

These are initially globular plants but with time gradually become columnar up to about 1 foot (30cm) tall and about 4 inches (10cm) in diameter. These plants have a depressed crown and spiralling ribs that are distinctly tuberculate. Their spination is quite variable but mostly pale brown to golden and pronounced.

This cactus usually takes 3–4 years to reach flowering size.

These are unusual plants, as they will produce 2–4 flowers at a time from their upper areoles. These can be pale yellow, dark yellow, yellow with a red throat or all red, but these forms do not seem to be stable when grown from seed.

Easy to grow from seed, but not particularly-fast growing, these usually take 3–4 years to reach flowering size.

Rebutia perplexa

The flowers that this cactus produces are often enough to completely hide the body.

This is a charming, small-growing species with many heads little larger than pea size. It makes a dense, small mound of heads with short ginger spines and produces delicate pink flowers about an inch (2.5cm) in diameter in the spring, often enough to hide the plant.

Like many of the small-growing species, it is comparatively slow, taking several years to fill a 3 inch (7.5cm) pot. An old plant could be contained in a 5 inch (12cm) one.

It prefers well-drained compost, as it can loose its roots and rot if kept wet constantly.

Rebutia pygmeae

This is one of a small group of what used to be called Digitorebutia, which is now mostly included in this species. These are small-growing plants, mostly with a tuberous base from which several to many short, finger-like stems arise.

As so many of the old Rebutia species of this type are now included here, it is very variable. Many have dark-colored bodies, some do not have central spines but most have a round areole.

Flowers are produced from the sides of the plants and are slightly less than an inch (2.5cm) in diameter. They can be almost any color from white, cream, yellow, and orange to shades of red and crimson.

These are easy plants to grow from seed. Their short, finger-like stems will flower when 2–3 years old in the spring.

The finger-like stems of this plant make it distinctive.

Rebutia steinbachii ssp. tiraquensis

This is another of the old Sulcorebutia species, which is now considered very variable with numerous synonyms.

These plants have small, ribbed heads and most have stout central spines up to an inch (2.5cm) long in some forms. Most offset freely to make clumps and usually the depressed crown of the plant lacks spines, which are produced later. The spine color varies from white to black through various yellows, red, and brown.

The flowers are usually in the bright red to violet spectrum.

This species is fairly distinctive as its plants normally have numerous rounded offsets and are noticeably spiny, although most plants seem to have little else in common. Its flowers are mostly in the red to violet spectrum.

There are currently four subspecies and *ssp. tiraquensis* is probably one of the most distinctive with its dark body, red spines, and bright red flowers.

As seed was not available from most of the old Sulcorebutia species (really just clones), many of these are propagated by cuttings. If the offsets are detached in the early spring and then dried for a little, many root down during the next couple of months.

Rhipsalis eliptica

The Rhipsalis are various shapes, many have cylindrical stems, some have angular ones, and a few have flat stem sections rather like an Epiphiphyllum. They are all eventually pendent epiphytes and most flower during the winter to spring period. The flowers are small, usually a half inch (1cm) or less and mostly cream to pale pink. They make small, globular, berry-like fruits that are green to white, to red when ripe. They are very sticky when opened.

Rhipsalis eliptica has flat stem segments, usually produced in clusters of 3–4 at the ends of the old stems. The sections arc up to about 6 inches (14cm) long and 1–2 inches (2.5–5cm) broad. These are quite variable in their dimensions. Most are dark green, often tinged with red in a bright situation. The whitish flowers are produced with up to five flowers per areole, which are followed by red seed pods. Like most Brazilian plants, they will not tolerate low temperatures and 50°F (10°C) is recommended. Plants should not be allowed to dry out completely during the summer, and they will need the occasional light watering during winter.

This cactus produces flattened Epiphyllum-like stems.

Rhipsalis floccosa ssp. tucumanensis

This Rhipsalis is one of the more robust of the cylindrical stemmed species. Its stems are initially erect but later pendent and often colors with red streaks. The areoles are pronounced and sunken and its flowers are large, a little over an inch (2.5cm) in diameter.

This is a fairly distinctive species and the various sub-species are only marginally different. *R. floccosa ssp. tucumanensis* has slightly larger fruits and the stems do not become red.

An easy species to grow, it requires a good-sized hanging basket. The pendent stems can easily grow to 6 feet (2m) or more in length.

The thick cylindrical stems flower in late winter.

Rhipsalis teres

This is a fairly common species in cultivation and has many synonyms for plants that are just slightly different.

It is a multi-branched, bushy plant that makes some strong, long branches, which later usually branch with 3–6 new stems at their tips. These stems then continue to branch and rebranch.

These long stems are initially erect but later become bent under the weight of the growth from their tips, giving the plants a distinctive appearance. The main growths are shorter, slender, fresh green stems, which produce numerous small cream flowers along the newer stems in the spring.

This is an easy plant to grow and will soon make fine clumps. It is a little more tolerant of lower temperatures than many species.

This plant is more tolerant of lower temperatures than many Rhipsalis.

Schlumbergera

This genus includes the Christmas cactus (or winter-flowering cactus of the Southern Hemisphere). These plants are natives of Brazil and have short flat-

tened stem segments like leaves with or without notches at the edges of the stems, in which can be found very small areoles. The stems branch from their tip, often making several new shoots at a time.

These plants grow from spring until autumn, when they make their numerous buds from the tips of their stems. Flowers can be produced anytime between early autumn and late spring. The plants need a bright situation to grow well but not full summer sun. They should be fed well during the summer to build them up for their flowering period.

There are now numerous hybrids available and it is not known whether the originally collected species is still in cultivation or not. The zygomorphic flowers (meaning their tops are longer than the bottom) are pollinated by humming birds.

The original plants were very much more pendent plants than today's upright hybrids. There is now a vast array of flower shape, color, and size.

This cactus is very popular as a house plant.

Stenocactus coptonogonus

Stenocactus is a strange and confused genus. It appears to be very closely related to Ferocactus, and this species is extremely close to *F. macrodiscus* and is not typical of the rest of the genus. For a long time, this genus was known as Echinofossulocactus, but this name has now been rejected.

The plants in each species are extremely variable and this has given rise to many different names that have now been amalgamated. The mostly large number of ribs have few, widely, spaced areoles with central, straight or curved, spines that are often flattened and pointing upwards with radial spines pointing downwards.

Stenocactus coptonogonus is different in that it only has 10–15 ribs and grows to about 4 inches (10cm) in diameter and up to about 5 inches (12cm) tall

This cactus has less ribs than most in this genus.

with age. This is the type species and if transferred to Ferocactus would invalidate the genus. Stenocactus are easy plants to grow but comparatively slow to become large plants. Seedlings of more than about an inch (2.5cm) will flower during the spring. Like most Stenocactus, the flowers have narrow petals usually with a darker mid rib. The flowers on this species are pale and dark pink, and about an inch (2.5cm) in diameter.

Stenocactus multicostatus

A very distinctive species, this has up to about 120 very narrow and wavy ribs, usually with only one areole per rib. The plants are flattened globose and bright green in color. The central spines are usually papery and flattened, and often slightly curved.

This is a very variable species with many ribs.

This is quite a variable species, both as to spination, and to the number of ribs. There are numerous plants that fit this species but at first glance appear quite distinct. It is a comparatively easy species to grow, but rather slow. Its flowers are whitish with a purplish to violet mid vein.

Stenocactus obvallatus

This species usually has a solitary body, larger than some species, which grows 2–5 inches (5–12cm) in diameter. It has 30–50 ribs that are swollen at the areoles, usually with 2–4 areoles per rib.

These plants have an upward-pointing, central spine that is wide and flattened and up to 2 inches (5cm) long and reddish brown in color. Their other central spines are a similar color and their radial ones shorter and white. The pale flowers have a deeper reddish mid vein. Like all Stenocactus, these plants are quite variable.

This species has flat, flexible spines.

Stenocactus vaupelianus

This species is quite distinctive with its pale spines, but can be individually quite variable.

This is a fairly distinctive species. Its plants are globose and up to about 4 inches (10cm) in diameter. The general appearance of these plants is a covering of white to golden radial spines, with a woolly crown and yellow flowers. Individually, these plants are quite variable but all have this general appearance. Their central spines are usually erect or curved upwards and shades of golden brown to black.

These plants will usually flower when about an inch (2.5cm) in diameter at about 2–3 years old from seed. This is an easy species to grow and flower.

Thelocactus bicolor

This is the most widespread species of this genus and grows from Texas to northern Mexico. Being so widespread, it is also extremely variable in the wild and has many different forms.

It usually has a solitary plant body (or forms clumps of smaller heads) and can grow quite large, up to 15 inches (36cm) tall and 7 inches (17cm) in diameter. Often the plant bodies narrow as they become taller, giving them a pear shape. The spines are extremely variable from curved slender spines to broad flattened ones, from red to yellow to brown. Their central spines are usually much more prominent than their radial ones. They produce large flowers, 2–3 inches (5–7cm) in diameter, that are a bright magenta, sometimes shaded and sometimes with a frilly edge to the petals. They are fairly distinctive, which makes identification of a flowering plant reasonably easy.

The spines are extremely variable from curved slender spines to broad flattened ones.

These plants are beautiful, even when small, and they will flower when only about 2 inches (5cm) in diameter, at about 2–4 years old from seed. They are not, however, the easiest of plants to grow successfully. They seem to need a slightly higher temperature, minimum 50°F (10°C), and are prone to rot if not grown in a free-draining compost.

Thelocactus heterochromus

This cactus is characterized by its bright flowers.

These plants are usually solitary and are flattened, globose plants, blue-green in color and up to about 3–4 inches (7.5–10cm) tall and 6 inches (14cm) in diameter. They have 7–11 ribs, which are notched into large, rounded tubercles. The star-like spines are up to about an inch (2.5cm) in length and are pale colored, but often banded with red.

Large, magenta flowers up to about 4 inches (10cm) in diameter are produced in summer making this a distinctive species. This is not a difficult plant to grow from seed, but is quite slow-growing.

Thelocactus hexaedrophorus

This species is vaguely similar to *Thelocactus heterochromus* and is much the same color. However, the body of the plant is much more hemispherical and its ribs are not pronounced, the large tubercles blending in to each other. The main difference is its 2 inch (5cm) diameter white flowers, which may have magenta mid veins.

These are quite easy plants to grow, but they have tuberous roots that can make them more prone to rotting in wet conditions. Seedlings will flower when about 2 inches (5cm) in diameter at about 3–4 years old from seed. This species needs to be repotted regularly, as the tuberous root can easily fill a pot at which point the top will stop growing.

This species needs to be repotted regularly.

Thelocactus macdowellii

This is probably the most distinctive of the Thelocactus and it was previously included in Echinomastus.

It grows to about 6 inches (14cm) tall and up to about 5 inches (12cm) in diameter, giving it a short columnar appearance. The plants have numerous small

This plant is well worth cultivating for its general shape and color.

tubercles, which are densely covered in white spines, almost obscuring the plant body. The 2 inch (5cm) diameter magenta flowers are mainly produced in spring, with a few in summer. It is a fairly slow-growing plant from seed and, although it seems able to tolerate lower temperatures down to at least 42°F (18°C), it can be prone to rotting if kept wet. Use a well-drained compost for the best results.

This is a very attractive, white, spined plant and is well worth cultivating, even if only for its general shape and color.

Thelocactus rinconensis

This flattened, globose species grows up to 8 inches (19cm) or more in diameter in the wild and about 6 inches (14cm) tall. These beautiful gray-bodied plants have quite pronounced tubercles and long spines. Old spines tend to soften and break down to become fibrous, a distinctive characteristic.

These cacti eventually grow to be quite large.

There are many forms of this species, which are quite variable, but quite similar in appearance. Seedlings take some while before they take on their full mature characteristics. When small they appear almost globular with much less pronounced tubercles.

These are not difficult plants to grow. By the time they have reached about 3 inches (7cm) in diameter, they are beautiful plants with blue-gray bodies.

Succulents

Aeonium arboreum

Most Aeoniums are native of the Canary Islands. The various species are localized according to which island they grow on, so can vary from tall solitary plants to small and bushy ones. In all of these species, the growing point of the plants turns into the flower head and, after flowering, the head dies. With those species that do not branch, this means the plant will die after flowering.

Aeonium arboreum is a popular tall-growing species that branches freely near the crown to make bushy plants. In cultivation, the bright green rosettes grow to about 5 inches (12cm) in diameter and the plants flower in the spring when about 3 feet (1m) tall. Like many Aeoniums, they have a pyramidal head of many, small, yellow flowers. The plants tend to be semi-dormant in mid-summer, shed-

The bush-like form of this species makes them popular as patio plants.

ding their lower leaves to go through the hottest months as terminal rosettes of thicker and smaller leaves. In the autumn, when they start to grow again, the rosettes will grow larger and a little more open as the stems elongate, until the following spring when the process repeats. During the hotter months, these plants will often make quite dense arial roots from the upper stems. These are soft and hair-like, but when they reach the soil they will begin to thicken and harden and make slender legs to support the upper part of the plant.

'Schwarzkopf' has almost black leaves.

In higher latitudes, these plants will grow well in full sun, and make attractive patio plants, or can be used for summer bedding. When grown outdoors for the summer, they become a much more robust plant. In lower latitudes with a high all-year temperature, they will do best with some shade. Succulents should be watered in the same way as cacti during the summer months and liberally in the spring and autumn. During the winter, water as soon as their leaves begin to droop. If given too much water in winter, the plants will become very drawn and weak.

Several forms of this species exist. There is a variegated form with yellow stripes on its leaves. This form seems to need more shade or its leaves burn up in the hot sun. The two most popular forms are f. *atropurpurea* and f. *schwarzkopf*, the purple and the black form. Both are very similar, although the f. *atropurpurea* has a tendency to revert to green during the poor light of winter, the color returning in the spring. All are very easy to propagate from cuttings.

Aeonium undulatum

The rosettes can be up to about a foot (30cm) in diameter.

This tall-growing species can grow to 5 feet (1.5m) tall and is normally unbranched, although plants will produce a limited number of new shoots from the base. After flowering, with large heads of small creamy yellow flowers, the stems will normally die right down to ground level.

The rosettes are terminal and compressed at the tips of stems. They can be up to a foot (30cm) in diameter. The newer and smaller leaves in the rosette usually have an undulating margin.

This is an easy species to grow, usually from a basal cutting, but it takes several years to grow to flowering size.

Agave americana

This popular and spectacular plant is widely cultivated throughout the world as a landscape plant in frost-free areas and as a potted or feature plant in cooler areas.

It is a large-growing species, up to 12 feet (4m) across with long, blue-gray leaves, which are reflexed above the middle. The plants cluster freely from the base and eventually the main rosette will flower with a 20–30 feet (6–9m) tall flower stem. After flowering, the rosette will die, although this may take several years.

This smaller growing variegated form is popular as a feature plant.

This species is comparatively hardy and will tolerate occasional light frosts, provided that it is kept comparatively dry. Propagate it with offsets from the parent plant, which normally will already have an independent root system. This is an easy plant to grow and well worth it if space is available.

The variegated form of this species is more popular as a potted plant, as it is slower to grow and not so large. It is not as hardy as the blue form, and needs a frost-free environment.

Agave filifera

The dense rosettes of this almost stemless species offset freely to make large clumps. Its narrow, bright green leaves, have a fibrous edge that breaks away into white filaments.

This is an easy plant to grow and makes an attractive potted plant, both for the greenhouse, and as an outdoor feature plant for garden use during frost-free months. Grow it in free-draining compost in half-depth pots. During the summer, potted plants outdoors will need very little maintenance, and should be watered occasionally during periods of drought. Plants are usually propagated by division.

When a parent plant is repotted, some of its offsets can be removed to make new plants. Larger offsets will already have an established root system. These can be potted and treated as established plants.

The edges of the leaves break up into fibers.

Agave parryi

This outstandingly beautiful species makes medium-sized plants up to 3–4 feet (1–1.2m) in diameter. Its broad gray-green to blue-green leaves are very compact and tipped with a dark spine. It is a fairly hardy species and may survive outdoors in areas with only occasional light frosts.

It is a fairly slow-growing species and the larger it becomes, the more beautiful it isl. Although it is reputed to offset freely, it can be very slow to do so. It is easy to grow from seed if any can be obtained. It probably takes ten years to grow to its full adult size and characteristics and (fortunately) many years to reach flowering size.

This is a superb species to use as a feature plant or in favored areas as a landscape plant.

The Agave is one of the most beautiful.

Agave parviflora

This beautiful species is much more suitable in size for those who have to protect their plants from the elements.

It makes rosettes of narrow, linear leaves up to about 8 inches (19cm) in diameter. It usually suckers freely to make clumps. The edges of its leaves are white and fibrous and the fibers break away to festoon the plant.

This species only grows to a small size.

This is an easy plant to initially grow from seed and then propagate by removing some offsets. It seems to take 5–10 years to reach flowering size, when it produces a 3–5 feet (1–1.8m) tall flower stem. After flowering, the rosettes will die. It is therefore useful to have at least one of two reserve plants of different sizes also growing.

It is not a difficult plant to grow, but will not tolerate very low temperatures or wet and boggy conditions. Grow it in well-drained compost and endeavor to keep a minimum of 42°F (5°C) temperature. Water freely in summer and keep dry in winter.

Agave stricta

This species has long narrow leaves rather like reeds. The end of each leaf turns into a very sharp-pointed spine. The dense rosette of leaves almost makes a ball shape and grows to about 4 feet (1.2m) in diameter. After flowering, it is one of the comparatively few Agaves that branch and produce one or more new heads. This plant can eventually, with great age, grow up to about 6 feet (2m) long.

It makes a superb feature plant, providing it can be placed where it does not come in contact with people, due to its very sharp spines.

This species is normally grown from seed, as offsets are seldom produced. Although not a difficult plant to grow, it can be slow in the first few years until it is well-established. It will tolerate cool conditions if kept dry but

This species has long needle-like leaves.

young plants are prone to rotting in cool, damp winters. Grow in well-drained compost and keep it dry in winter.

Agave victoria reginae

This beautiful, slow-growing species is very variable. The classic form is probably a large ball of incurved leaves that spiral in toward the center of the plant.

These plants have fairly short, broad, thick leaves loosely arranged in spirals around the crown. The leaves are marked on top and underneath with white line

This species is very slow growing.

markings. The tips of the leaves are rounded and have a short, hard spine. Most plants, when young, have leaves that point out straight from the crown of the plant. On large old plants, some forms will begin to curve their leaves upward to take on the classic ball shape.

Plants are normally grown from seed, as few offsets are usually produced. They are slow, and prone to rotting if kept too wet. It seems to take about 30 or more years for the plants to reach flowering size. Plants prefer a minimum of 42°F (5°C) in winter otherwise marking of the leaves can occur due to rot, or worse, the whole plant can rot. This is an outstanding plant and suitable for most collections, as it takes many years before it will outgrow even a limited space.

Aichryson x aizoides f. variegata

The Aichrysons are closely related to the Aeoniums, but are generally smaller more bushy plants. They also come from the Canary Islands and Madeira.

Aichryson x aizoides is probably better known as *Aichryson domesticum,* which is a plant not known to grow in the wild and is thought to probably be a hybrid. It is an easy plant to grow and roots readily from cuttings. It makes a small bush, which with poor light, makes a very lax plant. Given a bright situation and moderate amounts of water it soon grows quite large and makes a natural bonsai shape. If a lax plant is planted in a wide bowl, much deeper than before, then the stems touching or below soil will soon root down and make an attractive multi-stemmed plant.

This makes a very popular house plant.

These plants will grow to about 4–5 inches (10–12cm) tall and up to about one foot (30cm) in diameter. During the spring, some or all of their stems will produce clusters of small yellow flowers. As these are terminal on the stems, these will die back. It is seldom that all the stems flower at the same time. After flowering, the dead stems should be cut back and new branches will appear from below the cuts. These make attractive plants for inclusion in a small cactus garden, on their own or in hanging baskets.

The variegated form is attractive with its cream and white leaves, as well as dark green ones. All forms need to be propagated from cuttings. Keep them out of full summer sun, as the small leaves on the plants can easily "cook."

Aloe arborescens

The Aloes are a large group of rosette succulents mostly from Africa. They range in size from stemless rosettes little more than an inch (2.5cm) in diameter to trees 30 feet (9m) or more tall with rosettes of leaves at the tips of their stems.

Aloe arborescens is a bush-forming species, growing up to about 9 feet (2m) in old established plants and clumping to make large plants. They are usually dense and develop numerous new rosettes along older stems. These can grow to 3–4 feet (1–1.2m) long. There is also a variegated form with long yellow stripes down the leaves.

Unlike the Agaves, the Aloes do not have long fibers in their leaves and these can be easily broken. The juice of the Aloes have good medicinal properties when applied externally. This species is very easy to grow and soon makes quite large clumps if given a free root run. Plants normally flower with their bright orange-red spikes of flowers in late winter to early spring. Like almost all Aloes, they will not tolerate their leaves being frozen. Often plants grown outdoors, subjected to cold spells, will regenerate from lower down, or from the root stock. They will need a little water during winter, particularly when making their buds or the tips of the flower stems will not develop.

When given a free root run, this species produces quite large clumps.

Aloe aristata

No group of plants is complete without its exceptions. This is perhaps the most cold tolerant of all the Aloes. It will tolerate the occasional light frost if kept dry. It is an attractive, stemless, rosette plant, which grows to perhaps 6 inches (14cm) in diameter in some forms, and offsets profusely to make large clumps. Its 1 foot (30cm) tall flower stems are produced in spring and sometimes in summer.

This species grows during the spring and autumn. During the summer, if grown in full sun, it shrivels a little and the leaves curve inwards to protect the crown, making a ball shape. The normally thick and turgid dark green leaves become thin and flexible and a reddish color.

This species grows reasonably quickly, making many new leaves during the course of a year, and shedding the old bottom leaves as dried remains. This results in the situation where the bases of old clumps are sitting in their own leaf mold. This tends to keep the bases of the plants much drier

This semi-hardy species is easy to grow and flower.

so that often they will have very little growth. It is a good idea from time to time to repot these clumps and remove as much as possible of the old dried remains from underneath.

This is a very popular plant and is widespread in cultivation, probably due to its near indestructibility. It is easy to grow and easy to flower and should be included in every collection. Propagation is normally from offsets, which are usually already rooted.

Aloe ferox

This Aloe grows to be quite large and has distinctive spiny blue leaves.

This is a large-growing tree species with stems that eventually reach up to about 15 feet (5m). Its terminal rosette of broad blue toothed leaves is up to about 6 feet (2m) across. It is quite a variable plant and will flower when about 3 feet (1m) tall. The branched flower stem produces red to orange flowers.

Propagation is from seed, and the seedlings initially grow with their leaves arranged in a fan shape. When a little larger, the leaves begin to rotate into the typical rosette form. The broad blue, spiny leaves make this an attractive potted plant at any size. It is also very attractive as a landscape plant in frost-free areas.

An easy plant to grow, it simply requires normal treatment. However, it will not tolerate near freezing temperatures.

Aloe humilis

This is a small-growing plant with stemless rosettes up to about 4 inches (10cm) in diameter. It offsets freely to make clumps of broad bluish, spiny leaves. In the spring, it produces one foot (30cm) tall flower stems with bright orangey-red flowers.

This is a pretty, small growing species that flowers easily and is well worth growing. It will clump up to make a very attractive plant in say a 10 inch (25cm) pan. It has several different forms with slightly different leaf shapes, but all are attractive.

This is an easy plant to grow and is normally propagated by the division of some of the offsets, which are normally already rooted. This species seems quite tolerant of either

The small clumps of this plant flower in spring.

full-sun or shade. It requires a little water through the winter to encourage it to produce its flower stems. Like any of the succulents, it is better to try and maintain a minimum of 50°F (10°C) if plants are watered in winter.

Aloe variegata

Despite this being a common and very old species in cultivation, it is not one of the easiest plants to grow. Its boat-shaped leaves are strongly keeled and arranged in a triangular spiral. The leaves are banded with white markings. Flowers are produced in the spring on short flower stems.

This succulent is a popular house plant.

It seems that this plant is best grown on a windowsill by someone who knows nothing about it, not even that it is even a succulent. Given to a cactus collector, it suddenly becomes difficult to keep alive and often rots. The problem is that the plants like a fairly dry summer and a little water in winter, which is their main growing time. Cactus collectors tend to keep it too wet in summer and dry in winter.

Plants are usually propagated by removing some of the offsets from the base of the plant. It can be grown from fresh seed, but it is not often available.

Aloinopsis schooneesii

This small-growing member of the Mesembryanthemum family (Aizoaceae) makes an underground tuber from which short shoots grow. Its small triangular brownish leaves grow close to the ground and eventually it becomes about 5 inches (12cm) in diameter, densely covered in short, brownish-gray leaves.

This specimen is very old and has a large underground tuber.

Half-inch (1cm) diameter flowers are produced from autumn to spring and are yellow to pink with a red mid-vein. This is a charming little plant and unlike any other species. It is a fairly slow-growing species and can be prone to rotting. It requires a gritty well-drained compost. It seems to tolerate temperatures down to 42°F (5°C) in winter if kept dry.

Anacampseros rufescens

A small-growing, tuberous rooted plant, with tight rosettes of small swollen leaves, it will grow to about 2 inches (5cm) tall. However, as the stems are lax these spread out sideways to form a small clump. The small swollen leaves are a dark green on the upper side and reddish on the underside. Growing from each leaf axil is a small tuft of white hair.

The flowers of this species are borne on short shoots from the tips of the stems and are about ⁄ inch (1cm) across and light carmine in color. These flowers open only for a couple of hours in late afternoon. This plant is self-fertilizing and the small seedpods are like little papery brown wine glasses when ripe, and open at the top to expose the numerous seeds. The slightest breeze or knock will scatter these to the ground.

The flowers only open for a couple of hours in the afternoon.

This is an easy and interesting plant to grow from seed and will flower when about a year old. It seems tolerant of most things except gross over watering.

Argyroderma

This small-growing Mesembryanthum has a pair of semi-united light gray leaves and looks like a split green egg. The name when translated means "silver skinned." The plants in this genus are all fairly similar in shape and variable in flower color. They will flower in the autumn when about 2 years old. The flowers are white, red, violet, or yellow and about an inch (2.5cm) in diameter.

An example of some of the different forms of this mimicry plant.

This interesting group of plants tend to go dormant during the height of summer and come back into growth in the autumn when they flower. They are slow to make clumps and most do not usually have many heads. Their skin is hard to the touch and often when the plants absorb water, it splits. This is not unusual even in the wild. As these plants produce new leaves each year, and the old ones transfer their goodness to the new ones before shrivelling, any disfigurement is very temporary.

Like most of the highly succulent dwarf Mesembryanthemums, these plants are probably better grown in pots or pans, even where suitable conditions occur. During the winter, these plants seem able to tolerate low temperatures, above freezing, provided they are dry. At high temperatures they need the occasional light watering.

Beaucarnea recurvata (Nolina recurvata)

The large majestic pony tail plant.

The ponytail palm is a tall-growing plant with a large swollen trunk. It is related to the Yuccas and Agaves, but recently has been transferred to a new plant family known as Nolinaceae.

This plant is attractive at any size and makes an ideal feature plant, whether in a pot or as a landscape plant in a frost-free area. A seedling has a swollen base rising to a short stem that is crowned with a head of slender, flexible, narrow leaves. It will keep this shape for some while but as it grows, the base expands to a considerable diameter and it grows taller, up to about 30 feet (9m). The base narrows toward the taller stems, which have a large head of long, grass-like leaves. These stems branch freely from the trunk and make numerous heads. Unlike some of the Yuccas, if this species grows too tall, it can be pruned back hard, even back to the main trunk and numerous new shoots will soon develop again.

This species is known to have flowered at about 5 feet (1.5m) tall and at 15 years old but normally it needs to be much larger than this before it will flower.

It is an easy plant to grow from seed, but larger plants are usually available in the horticultural trade.

Cheiridopsis denticulata

This small genera of Mesembryanthemums are mostly small-clumping to ground cover plants with blue-green leaves. Most have a flat upper surface and a rounded lower one. Pairs of leaves are united at their bases around the stems.

The leaves on this species are up to 4 inches (10cm) long and united for about one-third of their length. Each stem has 2–3 pairs of leaves. The newest pair of leaves form a cone until fully developed before separating. They are bluish green in color and are flat on the upper surface, keeled below but becoming rounded.

These plants are easy to grow from seed and are better known as *C. candidissima*.

The plants branch to make clumps and produce cream to yellow flowers in the spring about 2 inches (5cm) in diameter. These are easy plants to grow from seed and will flower after a couple of years.

Cheiridopsis pillansii

The short swollen leaves of this species are blue-green to pale green. Its leaves are swollen at the base, thinning toward the top and rounded at the tips. A pair

of leaves are united at the base and usually the upper surfaces of each pair of leaves are held together until new leaves are produced. In outline, it is similar in shape to *Conophytum bilobum*.

Plants of this kind clump up freely, growing and flowering normally in the spring. During the summer, the old leaves gradually shrivel away to leave heads of a single pair of leaves.

There are several forms of this species with various leaf sizes, and all make attractive potted plants. They will eventually make clumps up to a foot (30cm) or more in diameter.

An example of the larger leaves of the form 'Crassa.'

Cheiridopsis purpurea

This attractive, small, blue, green-leafed species has swollen leaves with a distinct chin at the tip. Its thick leaves are flat on the upper surface and rounded on the underside. The leaves are roughly the same thickness through the upper part. These plants clump up easily, to make quite large plants that flower easily with purple flowers in the spring. This is an unusual color in this genus, as most Cheiridopsis have cream to yellow flowers.

This species is easy to grow from seed or from cuttings. The latter root easily during the summer months.

One of the few species in this genera with purple flowers, shown here just about to bloom.

Conophytum bilobum

This charming genus of the Mesembryanthums is one of the few in which you can have an almost complete collection on a windowsill. Until some recent studies were completed, the identification of plants in this group was very difficult.

One of the most variable of all the Conophytums.

Almost every habitat had slightly different forms that had given rise to a large number of names. The largest group of these similar species was those with tall, swollen bodies, and pairs of leaves having rounded tips and being laterally compressed. Nearly all of these had yellow flowers. Most of them are now considered forms of *C. bilobum*, which in turn is now very varied and yet all the plants have great similarities.

This is probably one of the easiest of the Conophytums to grow, and flowers between mid-summer and autumn. Most Conophytums have a summer dormant period, but *C. bilobum* seems capable of growing throughout most of the year. They should be treated much the same as cacti are during most of the year, but they do need watering a little later in the autumn so that they go through the winter in a turgid state.

Conophytum minutum

Despite its name, this is not one of the smallest Conophytums. This plant is composed of pairs of leaves united for most of their length except for a "mouth" in the top. The leaves are rounded like very small, slightly squashed peas, and form clumps. In the autumn, after they awake from their summer dormancy, the bodies will swell and burst through their papery skins. Shortly afterwards they will produce small, bright, pink flowers.

This plant needs a little water during winter, in all but the coldest weather, so it can stay turgid. In the spring, it will continue to stay green and turgid until early summer. Suddenly, within just a few days, the old leaves will shrivel to a papery skin, which will cover the plant until it awakens again in early autumn. Those heads that have flowered the

This is not the smallest of the Conophytums despite its name.

previous year will have divided into two heads. During its dormant period this plant should be watered occasionally or it will desiccate.

This is a small-growing plant and will take several years to outgrow a 2 inch (5cm) pot. A large old plant is perhaps 3–4 inches (7.5–10cm) in diameter.

Conophytum uviforme

This is a small, round-headed species with speckled leaves. It is a very variable species but is night-flowering and has white flowers with very spidery petals. Its small heads soon make a domed mound. It is a fairly easy plant to grow.

This attractive species can be grown from seed or propagated from cuttings. It will go to rest in late spring and its leaves will shrivel to a papery sheath. A little water is required from time to time during the summer or its stems will desiccate.

This is an extremely variable species that produces white flowers.

When the height of the summer is over and temperatures begin to cool, it is a good idea to give all Conophytums a good soak in early autumn. Within a week many will have come back into growth and the new leaves will burst through the old papery sheaths. The plants can then be kept damp until late autumn, during which time they will grow and flower.

Conophytum wettsteinii

This is one of a comparatively small number of species that have a flat top, very reminiscent of being squashed. The heads on this species can be up to nearly an inch (2.5cm) in diameter, but are usually a little smaller. This plant normally grows so that all its heads are horizontal with the ground. Bright pink flowers are produced in mid autumn.

Although this is an easy plant to grow, it is a little less tolerant of over watering than some others.

When most of the Conophytums are in growth by mid autumn treat any that have not

This species has distinctly large flat heads.

revived with suspicion. There are just one or two that are much later growing, but generally any lack of growth will mean that the plants have lost their roots and their lower stems are dead. These plants should be pulled apart to make either a single head or small groups and dried for a week. These should then be put in a tray of gritty compost, pushed into the base of the leaves so that they can develop a new root system. Keep slightly damp and they can root down within a couple of weeks.

Cotyledon orbiculata and f. undulata

Cotyledon orbiculata is an exceedingly varied species with leaves that vary from slender and almost cylindrical to fat and chunky to round. These plants are bushy and can grow up to about 3 feet (1m) tall in some forms.

    Cotyledon orbiculata has mealy white leaves and is often seen in collections.

It makes a small bush up to about one foot (30cm) tall and offsets freely to make large clumps. Old stems are best removed from time to time in order to tidy the plant. Its flowers are red and bell-shaped and produced during the summer.

    The other attractive form is *undulata*, which also has mealy white leaves but with wavy edges. If this is grown in full sun, then its underlying leaves become a beautiful purple color. Like many of the Crassula family it does not like to be dry for any length of time in the summer or its leaves will shrivel and drop.

This is an extremely varied species, as f. *undulate* (top right) demonstrates with its wavy edged leaves.

    Most Crassula seed is very erratic in germination. The seed is mostly dust-like and sometimes only 1–2 percent will germinate. At other times it looks like about 150 percent. This is an easy species to propagate from cuttings.

Cotyledon tomentosa ssp. ladismithensis

This species grows into a bush about 1 foot (30cm) tall. It branches freely from along its stems, which are brown in color. Its leaves are swollen and hairy and olive green in color. The upper edge undulates and these are often a reddish hue. The plant is sometimes called the bear's paw plant.

The plants flower in the autumn with short terminal stems of small, cup-shaped flowers, yellowish orange in color.

This specimen is a new variegated form.

This is an easy plant to grow and attractive at any size. After flowering any dead flower stems should be removed. At the same time the plant can be tidied and any straggly stems cut away. These make ideal cuttings and root quite easily. After about 5–10 years, the plants become very woody at the base and at that time, it is best to start a new plant. The old one can be reduced to cuttings.

Crassula arborescens

The large blue leaves have red edges.

The Crassula family (Crassulaceae) is a large one and has numerous succulent plants in it, in many different genera. Crassula is also the name of one particular genus that numbers over 150 species and are mostly from the southern hemisphere. This small-growing species is about an inch (2.5cm) tall, while the largest is a bushy plant up to about 10 feet (3m) tall. Most plants of this genus are collected for their shape and succulent leaves. Although many will flower quite easily during winter, the flowers on most are not particularly spectacular.

Crassula arborescens is a large growing bushy plant up to about 6 feet (2m) tall. It usually has one main trunk, which is thick and swollen and covered in papery bark. The broad, rounded leaves are a blue-green in color and usually have a red edge. The old leaves are deciduous, mostly dropping in the spring. The leaves are thick and heavy and often weigh the branches down. It is a good idea in the spring to prune any very long branches back to a side shoot in order to keep the plant in a good shape. The prunings can be used as cuttings.

This is not one of the most floriferous Crassulas, but it will sometimes produce clusters of small pink flowers in the spring.

Crassula columella

This dwarf species will grow to about 6 inches (14cm) tall. Its short stems are densely packed with velvety leaves making short columns. The stems, initially erect, can become procumbent as they elongate. The plants branch freely to make clumps. Minute, tubular, cream flowers are produced in clusters from the tips of the stems on short stalks.

The dwarf clumping species will grow to about 6 inches (14cm) tall.

This is an easy-growing, miniature Crassula and one that propagates readily. It will grow best when not in full sun and kept regularly watered during the spring and summer.

Crassula deceptor

Another miniature Crassula that makes a short column of densely packed leaves, this is quite variable and can grow from 1–2 inches (2.5–5cm) in diameter. Its gray leaves make a four-sided column, which has numerous raised, dark green dots. It only branches very sparingly.

This species requires full sun and a dry winter rest. It is a pretty plant to grow and worth including in any collection.

The leaves on this succulent have unusual markings.

Crassula multicava

This short-growing species branches freely to make large clumps up to about 9 inches (21.5cm) tall. It will tolerate shade and is rapid-growing if kept damp and is used extensively as a groundcover plant in frost-free areas.

In the spring, it makes flower stems from the ends of its shoots about 4 inches (10cm) long and produces numerous small, red buds that open to pale pink flowers, rather reminiscent of a leafy saxifrage. After flowering, its heads produce numerous small bulbils, which drop and regenerate more plants. It is ideal for growing in a large container and very pretty in the spring.

It is a very easy plant to propagate. Apart from the bulbils, any short stem will soon produce roots and make a new plant. For rapid growth, grow it in the shade and keep damp. It will grow in the sun, but its leaves will lack the luster of one grown in the shade.

This species easily forms large clumps.

Crassula ovata (syn. Crassula argentea)

This small, tree-like species is often known as the money plant or friendship plant. It will grow to 10 feet (3m) or more in height. It has a main trunk that is thick and fleshy and grows up to about a foot (30cm) in diameter. Its bark is brown, which sometimes turns red when grown in full sun. The leaves are thick

and fleshy and when grown in a bright situation are often edged in red. Clusters of small, starry white flowers are produced during winter and, if the temperatures are not too high, then they will last for weeks.

Often this plant is seen as a poorly grown house plant, grown in poor light, in a compost that resembles concrete and a pot that is far too small. Consequently, the leaves are

The common name for this succulent is money plant or friendship plant.

often very small and the stems thin, limp, and pendent. These are plants that are quite quick-growing, like plenty of sunshine, plenty of water during summer, and to be well fed. Given this treatment, the leaves are large and glossy green, the branches sturdy and erect, and the plants look attractive. In higher latitudes, these plants will really benefit from being grown outdoors during the summer. In spring, it is worth pruning them if necessary. Any branches in the wrong place should be removed, any very long branches should be shortened, and basal shoots should be removed if it is desirable to keep a tree-like appearance. A pretty cultivar is 'Hummel's Sunset,' which when grown in full sun has a yellow margin to the leaf and a red edge. Grown in the shade, this is almost indistinguishable from the plain green form. These plants make ideal patio plants for summer, or can be used for hedging in frost free areas.

Crassula perfoliata f. falcata (syn. Crassula falcata)

This gray-leafed plant has long, narrow, curved gray leaves and these have given it the common name of propeller plant. This plant can be quite large growing and makes clumps that offset freely. The longer stems have a terminal inflorescence during summer that is a large cluster of small red flowers that are sweetly perfumed.

This is an old favorite and is often seen in collections. Unless grown in a very large container, it will need pruning each year to remove the old stems that have flowered, allowing the new ones to develop for the following year. The prunings can be used as cuttings to make new plants.

An easy plant to grow in either shade or sun, this should not be allowed to dry out for any great length of time during spring until autumn. Unless kept at a very high winter temperature, it should be kept almost dry.

The flowers of this plant are sweetly scented.

Crassula perforata

The bushes of this plant need pruning to keep in good shape.

This is another very variable species with numerous different forms. It is a straggling shrublet, growing to about a foot (30cm) or so tall. The stems will grow up to nearly 3 feet (1m) long but above about a foot (30cm), they become prostrate. These plants branch freely both from the base and from higher up the stems, particularly if they are damaged. The stems are very slender and quite brittle when young and pairs of leaves are united at their bases, as though they are threaded onto the stems.

Because the stems are so slender, from time to time some of them will collapse sideways under their own weight. These should be removed in order to keep the plant tidy. These stems can be cut into short sections and rooted down. Plant several together in a pot for an "instant" new plant.

This species grows best if it is not allowed to dry out for any length of time. It should occasionally be watered during the winter and although it needs a bright situation, is probably best kept out of full summer sun.

Crassula tetragona

These plants are woody shrublets, which growing up to about 3 feet (1m) tall. The stems are fairly slender and often collapse under their own weight, making a spreading bush. These plants have opposite pairs of leaves arranged alternately at right angles to each other. The leaves are small and almost cylindrical, narrowing towards the tip and united slightly at the base. These plants branch freely to make a bushy shape.

This species perhaps looks at its best when comparatively small. A plant that is branching, when about 3–4 inches (7.5–10cm) tall, looks just like a miniature tree. Any stems can be used as cuttings. These should be cut into sections, 2–3 inches (5–7.5cm) long and pushed into a tray of compost to root. Once rooted the cutting will branch usually with 3–4 stems and take on their tree-like appearance. These are ideal for anyone who wants to create a miniature garden.

Small plants are ideal for miniature arrangements.

Dioscorea elephantipes (syn. Testudinaria elephantipes)

This interesting winter-growing plant makes long, climbing vines with minute yellow flowers in the autumn. The stems die down again in the spring and the plant is dormant through the summer.

This old plant demonstrated the unusual "carved" base.

The interesting part of this plant is the base or caudex. It is large and swollen and will grow up to about 3 feet (1m) in diameter. Its surface appears wooden and is divided into several sided warts that are deeply fissured in between. It has the appearance of being carved out of wood.

This plant is not difficult to grow from seed sown in the autumn. During its first winter, it makes a small underground tuber. During the summer a dormant plant should be watered lightly from time to time. In late summer or early autumn it should be watered well and the vines will start to grow again. After 3–4 years, the caudex will begin to emerge above ground level. When this plant is repotted, it is important that the base of the plant is slightly buried as otherwise it will desiccate during the summer months. Do not over water it in winter, as the caudex is prone to rotting.

Dudleya britonii

The Dudleyas are fairly closely related to the Echeverias, and many are covered in a white mealy farina, which is very easy to rub off and will spoil the plants. This farina is the dried remains of wax excreted onto the leaves.

These plants make large solitary rosettes up to about 18 inches (43cm) wide and 4–6 inches (10–14cm) tall. The long narrow leaves are covered in white farina. It comes from Baja, California, and is fairly slow growing. It is not very common in cultivation, but well-grown plants make spectacular feature plants. They should be grown out of touching distance, as the farina is easily removed by touch and takes a long time to repair itself.

These plants should be grown in gritty, well-drained compost, as they can rot easily if kept wet.

Avoid touching this plant, as its silver leaves show every fingerrprint.

Echeveria agavoides

These plants in the wild are usually found at altitudes between 2,000 (610m) and 10,000 feet (3050m), and are mostly from Mexico, preferring shady areas and dry winters. They are rosette plants, many stemless, some growing up to about 3 feet (1m) tall, a few making small bushes. Most are cultivated for their shape

An example of the unusual crested form of this species.

and color, as many have attractive leaves. Some species are summer flowering, but many flower in the autumn and winter period.

Echeveria agavoides is a stemless rosette plant with thick, pointed, olive green leaves, sometimes tinged with a red edge or tip. The rosettes normally grow to 6–9 inches (14–21.5cm) diameter and offset slowly when mature. This is a very distinctive species and is well worth growing. It will tolerate full sun (at least in higher latitudes), provided that it is not kept in a dehydrated

This species has thick, chunky leaves.

state. Keep dry in winter and water freely in summer when dry. The flowers are small and insignificant.

The cristate form of this plant is often available and is no more difficult to grow that the ordinary form.

Echeveria derenbergii

This is a small-growing species, making short stems that offset freely to make clumps. The rosettes are normally 2–4 inches (5–10cm) in diameter and the leaves are blue-green, often tinged with red. The short flower stems are up to about 4 inches (10cm) tall in spring and produce attractive red and yellow tubular to bell-shaped flowers.

This is a very popular small growing species.

This is a popular species in cultivation and is one of the parents of a number of hybrids. It is an excellent plant for use in small decorative displays and cactus gardens. It is usually propagated by removing the offsets, which rapidly root down to make new plants.

Although it will tolerate full sun in higher latitudes, it will grow much better if protected from the full strength of the summer sun. It is an easy plant to grow and worthy of inclusion in most collections.

Echeveria gibbiflora

This is a taller growing species with a terminal rosette of leaves. It will grow to a foot (30cm) or more tall with a rosette 6 inches (14cm) or more in diameter. The broad leaves are very colorful with different shades of reddish green to purple.

This species eventually becomes top heavy and untidy and it is a good idea to behead the plant and reroot the top. The stems, which are usually solitary, will then often offset to make new rosettes.

The best time of year to propagate these plants is in the spring when it has warmed up after winter. Leave about 3 inches (7.5cm) of stem beneath the rosette and cut through the stem. Find a flowerpot that the rosette will sit on that is deep enough for the stem to hang free. Leave the pot empty and normally the rosette will make a root system in 3–4 weeks and can then be potted. Even if it has not produced roots, it can still be potted and will soon root down into gritty

The large rosettes eventually grow quite tall.

compost. This species is a little large for growing on a windowsill, but very colorful in a glasshouse or outdoors.

Echeveria harmsii

For such a small plant it has very large flowers.

This small bushy species grows to about 1 foot (30cm) tall and has a very lax terminal rosette of narrow green leaves. The leaves and stems are slightly puberulent (velvety) and are often tinged red at the margins and tips. The main beauty of this species is that the flowers are totally out of proportion to the plant. The flowers are up to about an inch (2.5cm) long, yellow with red margins down to the petals.

This is not a difficult plant to grow, but it is important to keep it in good condition. In the spring, which is its main growing period, it requires plenty of water and soon makes leaves and flowers. After it has flowered, if it is too dry, it tends to shed its leaves and leave just the bare stems with small leaves at the tips. It will tend to stay like this until the following spring. It is probably better to grow it as a houseplant, in a shady spot, and to keep it well watered during the summer. It is easy to propagate from cuttings in the spring.

Echeveria setosa

Echeveria setosa is a small branching species with very furry leaves, and makes rosettes from 2–4 inches (5–10cm) in diameter. It offsets freely and will eventually make short stems up to about 4 inches (10cm) tall. The flowers are produced on stems up to about one foot (30cm) long and are a very bright yellow and orangey red.

This is a very attractive species to grow and there are numerous hybrids with this species as one of the parents. The flowers are distinctive and very brightly colored. This species requires shade, as when grown in full sun, the leaves seem to get so hot that they "cook" and collapse. Like any plant with hairy leaves, water should be kept off the foliage in winter as it can cause rotting.

The smaller growing v. *ciliata* has brightly colored flowers.

Echeveria tolucensis

This species is very closely related to *Echeveria secunda* (*E. glauca*) and is little different, apart from its chromosome count. It makes almost stemless rosettes up to about 5 inches (12cm) in diameter of glaucous green leaves and offsets freely to make clumps.

This is an easy plant to grow and is very tolerant. *E. secunda* is often used as a summer bedding plant and used in floral clocks, etc. There is no reason why this species could not be used instead.

This species is often used as a summer bedding plant.

Euphorbia flanaganii

There are quite a number of different species of Euphorbia which have a central firm head, rather like a carrot, which is a little exposed from the ground. This species has a central column that is short, from which radiate numerous short green, slender shoots. These stems are deciduous, but in cultivation, a well-grown plant may keep most of them for several years, making a dense mass of stems. In the wild, where conditions are much harsher, these stems are comparatively short, but in cultivation, with better conditions these can become long and straggly.

This is an easy plant to grow and popular in cultivation. There is also a cristate form, which makes thin, crested stems, rather than a main head. Keep dry in winter at a minimum temperature of 50°F (10°C).

"Medusa Head" has long, trailing stems.

Euphorbia milii and cultivars

This spiny stemmed bush from Madagascar is perhaps one of the less succulent Euphorbia species. It is a leafy bush, and in cultivation there are now a great number of different hybrids, with a variety of leaf sizes, flower colors, and sizes.

This species has a crown of thorns.

The Euphorbias do not have true flowers; the colorful parts are the bracts, or modified leaves, and the floral parts are minute in the middle of the bracts. The plants vary in size from about 4 foot (1.2m) tall bushes to miniatures that will only grow a foot (30cm) or so tall. The leaves are also variable in shape, from small and almost round to larger and lanceolate. The traditional color for them was bright red, then yellow and later white, and now a wide range of colors and shades are available in this spectrum.

These are easy plants to grow as houseplants. They need a bright position, but not full summer sun. They prefer to be kept at about 70°F (21°C), although they will tolerate temperatures down to about 50°F (10°C). At lower temperatures, they will need to be kept dry and will shed their leaves and flowers. At higher temperatures, they will need to be kept watered and should stay in leaf and flower for most of the year. These plants are normally propagated from cuttings, although they are not the easiest to root.

Euphorbia obesa

This beautiful species is initially globular to hemispherical, but later becomes columnar. This plant can be temperamental to grow, but if it survives long enough may eventually grow to about 2 feet (60cm) tall. It is usually solitary, but occasionally the odd plant will produce off-sets from the base.

Euphorbia obesa prefers a dry winter temperature above about 50°F (10°C), as below this it is prone to rotting, even if kept dry. There is usually enough humidity in a glasshouse to cause this problem.

This succulent is initially globular, and looks a little like a tartan golf ball, before it becomes more columnar.

This is a beautiful plant and has about 6–10 ribs and banded markings on its stems. Most plants are unique and slightly different to the trained eye. It is either male or female flowered and these flowers are produced regularly throughout the summer months. Its very small flowers can easily be checked for sex; female ones have a star-like stigma in their centers, while the male ones have stamens and bright yellow pollen clusters.

During the summer, treat it as you would a cactus. They are slow-growing, but flower when quite young. Propagate from seed.

Euphorbia trigona

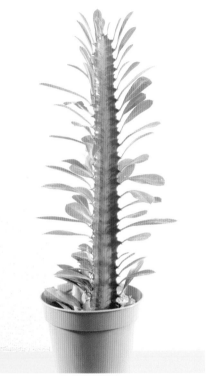

This large clumping bushy species is popular as a house plant.

This species is only known from cultivated plants. It is widely sold as a houseplant in higher latitudes and often used as a hedging plant in lower ones.

It has narrow triangular stems, often banded or marked with yellow. It offsets freely to make dense, tall bushes up to about 5 feet (1.5m) tall. The tips of the stems usually carry a few rudimentary leaves. The original plant is thought to have come from Angola, although India is often quoted as its origin.

There is also a purple form in which all the stems are tinted with deep red-purple shades; again it is very popular as a houseplant.

E. trigona is susceptible to rot at low temperatures and really needs at least 50°F (10°C) in winter. It will grow in full sun in summer, but often looks a little bleached. It is best given a little protection from full summer sun in a glasshouse. Propagate from cuttings, as it is never known to have flowered.

Faucaria tigrina

The tiger's jaw is a popular and pretty small-growing Mesembryanthum. Its individual heads are composed of several pairs of thick, chunky leaves which are narrowed toward the tip and have 9–10 small green wispy teeth along their edge. The bright yellow, 2 inch (5cm) diameter flowers are produced in the autumn–winter period. There are many different forms of this species, which has a variety of leaf shapes and sizes.

This species is very similar to *F. felina* but that normally has fewer teeth on the leaves.

This plant soon offsets to make clumps, which can grow to about 1 foot (30cm) in diameter. Eventually the old stems become very woody and cease to take up food and water properly, so it is best to reduce this plant to cuttings, which root easily and start again. Several cuttings placed in a pan will soon make a new clump.

The common name for this species is tiger's jaw.

Provided that this plant is kept dry in winter, it will tolerate temperatures down to near freezing. It seems to be still dormant in early spring but from late spring until late autumn it should be regularly watered when dry. Its growing season ends with the plant's flowering period.

An easy and attractive small plants to grow, it should be in every collection. Propagate from seed or cuttings.

Fenestraria rhopalophyllum

This species is commonly called baby's toes.

A charming miniature succulent Mesembryanthum, this has short cylindrical, erect, glossy green leaves with a window in the end. The plant will make new heads and cluster to make clumps perhaps up to 3 feet (1m) wide. Normally the old horizontal stems will rot away and their heads root down to make a cluster of plants.

This species, although not difficult to grow, is quite prone to rotting if kept wet. Use a gritty, well-drained compost and be sparing with water in the early part of the year. Its main growing season is from mid summer until late autumn and during this period it will flower freely. Its flowers are on 2–3 inch (5–7.5cm) long stems and are usually yellow or white. Some forms are a darker yellow, and possibly have a reddish tinge.

Keep it dry in winter. It is not unusual for this plant to shed many of its old leaves during its resting period. It is important that the plant is kept dry so that these dry away rather than rot off in a damp environment, or it can kill the whole plant.

Propagate from seed and it will flower at perhaps a year old.

Gasteria bicolor

This genus used to be included in the Lily family, but is now included in the Aloe family, Aloaceae, along with the other similar succulent plants.

This is a widespread genera from South Africa and it seems that every individual habitat has slightly different forms. This has given rise to numerous names that have now been reduced to 16 species. In cultivation, there are also believed to be many hybrids.

Gasteria bicolor is a species with shiny green leaves, often arranged in a distichous fan or a spiralled distichous fan, with the leaves often twisted sideways. Most have leaves that are flecked with prominent white markings.

The v. *liliputana* is a small-growing form of *G. bicolor*, with leaves up to 4–5 inches (10–12cm) long.

The v. *liliputana* is attractive and small growing.

Gasterias are easy plants to grow and very tolerant of neglect and low temperatures, although not freezing. They will not, however, tolerate long periods of wet conditions. Propagation is easy either from seed or by division; often the offsets will already have an independent root system.

Gasteria carinata

This is a widespread and very variable species in the wild and has many different forms. Most plants have slight raised dots and the skin feels rough to the touch.

Note the raised white dots on the leaves of v. *verrucosa*.

Most initially have their leaves arranged in a fan shape but older plants will become rosettes. The leaf shape is very variable, from long and keeled to short and rounded leaves.

One of the more popular Gasterias in cultivation is *G. carinata* v. *verrucosa*, which has pointed, dark green leaves with an oblique keel down one side of the leaf and a dense covering of raised white dots.

Like all the Gasterias, these are easy plants to grow and will tolerate shade or full sun, but not frost. The plants are mostly prolific in the way they offset to make large clumps.

The tall spikes of its flowers that are swollen in the middle are red and orange to green, and are produced from the spring to autumn. This genus gets its name from the flowers, which are supposed to look like stomachs.

Gibbaeum album

Gibbaeums are short, mat-forming Mesembryanthums. The plants have short internodes and the leaf pairs are united around the stem for part of their length.

These leaf pairs are unequal in length, one often having a chin, overlapping the other.

Gibbaeum album gets its name from the whitish green color of the leaves, which are short and swollen. The flowers are pink to white. This is a small-growing species, and makes clumps up to 6 inches (14cm) in diameter.

These pale-colored plants produce pink flowers.

These are relatively easy plants to grow, but need a well-drained, gritty compost. Most Gibbaeums need watering late into the autumn so that they are turgid during the winter as otherwise they do not flower in the spring. During the summer, the plants grow slowly and require much the same treatment as cactus do. These are easy to grow from seed and will flower when 3–4 years old. Plants are tolerant of low temperatures, but a minimum of 45°F (7°C) is recommended.

Gibbaeum heathii

This is another small-growing species that is quite variable. The almost united leaf pairs are almost egg-shaped, one leaf just slightly larger than the other. This is quite a variable species with both small heads and larger ones, up to about an

This species forms clumps and has swollen leaves.

inch (2.5cm) tall. This plant clusters freely and soon makes clumps. The flowers are white to pink and produced in the spring. A fairly rare plant in cultivation until fairly recently, it is now generally available.

It is not a difficult plant to grow but can be prone to rotting if kept in poorly drained compost. Its main growth is in the autumn to spring period, although it should be kept dry in the depths of cool winters. It is easy to grow from seed, but a little reluctant to flower as a seedling.

Gibbaeum schwantesii

This is a vigorous and large-growing species that makes mats. Its leaves are long and one of each pair is hooked at the tip. The leaves are soft and velvety to touch. Its flowers are 1–2 inches (2.5–5cm) in diameter and white to pale pink.

This species is very similar to *G. velutinum,* which has slightly longer leaves and a more purple flower.

This is an easy plant to grow and soon makes fine clumps. Plants grown from seed will flower when 1–2 years old. This species flowers quite prolifically in the spring and autumn.

This species forms large clumps.

Graptopetalum bellum (syn. Tacitus bellus)

This relatively recent introduction is closely related to the Echeverias. It has small dense rosettes of thin gray leaves, up to about 4 inches (10cm) in diameter. The short stems of large red flowers make this a very distinctive species.

It is still relatively uncommon in cultivation, as it is very prone to rotting in the winter due to high humidity. Moisture seems to get trapped in the rosette and it will suddenly rot off. A minimum temperature of 50°F (10°C) is recommended in winter and to keep it completely dry.

Like many of the Echeveria group this species can be propagated from leaves. De-pot the plant and turn it upside down, then carefully ease off sideways a few of the sound basal leaves. Place these upright in a very gritty compost and keep them slightly damp. Within 2–3 months, new little plants will grow from the base of the leaves.

For such a small plant it has unusually large flowers.

Graptopetalum paraguayense

This is a remarkably robust species and widely distributed in cultivation. It is very closely related to *G. amethystinum*. This plant is a small shrub, which rapidly become prostrate or pendent. It has a terminal rosette of pointed rose to lavender leaves. The leaves are very lightly attached to the stem and easily knocked off, but will rapidly produce new plantlets.

The fallen leaves of this plant soon make new plants.

This can be an untidy plant and it is best, from time to time, to remove the terminal rosettes with a short stem and to reroot them. Plant several together in a pan for an instant new plant.

This plant is very easy to grow and tolerant of low temperatures.

Haworthia attenuata

This is an attractive species with raised white dots.

The Haworthias are related to the Aloes and are now included in the family Aloaceae, but used to be included in the Lily family. These are small-growing rosette plants that produce tall spikes of small, white, semi-tubular flowers at most times of the year.

Haworthia attenuata is often wrongly depicted as *H. fasciata*, a much larger growing plant seldom seen in cultivation. It has many leaves that taper to a fine point in an almost stemless rosette. Its inner leaves are usually erect and the outer ones can be horizontal or upward pointing. The plant normally offsets freely to make large clumps. This is quite a variable plant in the wild and there have been many varieties and forms of it named in the past. The leaves have raised white markings like dots, which may be large or small, random, or in bands.

An easy plant to grow, it can be grown in the shade or sun, although some protection will be needed in lower latitudes. At higher latitudes, a plant that is grown in the shade will normally be dark green and grow throughout most of the year. It will tend to loose most of its roots during the dormant period, growing new ones as soon as moisture is available. If grown in full sun, it will take on hues of red-brown and may become dormant until the temperature drops.

Haworthia cymbiformis

This again is a very variable species and now embodies many of the old species that were similar in appearance. The plant has broad, pale green leaves that are usually about a third as thick as broad and has rosettes that can grow up to about 5 inches (12cm) on some forms, although 2–3 inches (5–7.5cm) is more

A very variable species with broad, soft green leaves, which soon make large clumps.

normal. The upper surface of the leaves is usually slightly concave and will become yellowish with orange tints when grown in full sun.

This is probably the easiest and most widespread Haworthia in cultivation, as, apart from being frozen, it is extremely tolerant of neglect and maltreatment. It is easy to propagate by detaching an offset, which will usually have an independent root system. This plant will grow into a large mound over the passage of a few years.

Haworthia limifolia

This beautiful and distinctive species has broad leaves that taper to a point. The leaves are usually dark in color, green, brownish-green, or reddish-green. Most forms have raised bands of dots across their leaves, rather like sand after the sea has receded. These plants are usually stoloniferous and will slowly make new plants a little distance from the parent plant if grown in a bed. In a pot, these will develop around the edge or through the drainage holes in the bottom.

This plant has unusual ribbed leaves.

This distinctive and beautiful species is not very fast growing, but is certainly one that is worth including in any collection. It is not difficult to grow and requires normal cactus treatment.

Haworthia maxima

This species has had many names in the past. It is perhaps better known as *H. margaritifera* or *H. minima*. It has, however, been found that both of those names have already been used for other plants, so it has been renamed again. As this is probably the largest-growing of the Haworthia species, the name of *H. minima* seemed most confusing. This was because it was originally thought to be an Aloe and therefore the name would have been appropriate. The new name,

H. maxima, makes much more sense.

This plant can grow to about 9 inches (22cm) tall and 3–4 inches (7.5 10cm) in diameter. Its thick, pointed leaves are broad at the base and covered in large raised white dots. The leaves are often incurved in the crown of the plant. Its flower stem is long and

These are very robust plants with thick leaves.

very robust, another distinguishing feature. This is a very distinctive species.

It is not one of the easiest of succulents to grow and is comparatively slow and does not like to be over watered. It is best grown in a very gritty compost and kept dry during the winter.

Haworthia truncata and v. maughanii

Of all the Haworthias, these are probably two of the most sought-after species. Both have truncate leaves, leaves that look as though they have been cut off just above ground level.

The leaves of *Hawthornia truncata* resemble stepping stones.

These two old species have been amalgamated, as they are both very similar. The plants of *H. truncata* have their leaves arranged in a fan, making the view from above appear like wide stepping-stones. These vary greatly in width, thickness, and markings. Those of *v. maughanii* are arranged in a spiral, making a circle. These two species are not the easiest to grow and are very variable. In fact, several hundred "forms" are available from some nurseries. The truncate leaves have "windows" in the top and in the wild this would be the only part visible. Both species have thick, fleshy roots that can pull the plants down into the soil. During periods of drought, it is not unusual for the plants to lose these roots completely. In cultivation, this is often after the winter rest.

These plants should be grown in a gritty, well-drained compost and watered sparingly at all times. This is a slow-growing species, but will in time create a clump.

Kalanchoe beharensis

This is a large-growing bush up to about 10 feet (3m) tall. It normally has large leaves up to 1 foot (30cm) long that are quite variable in shape, mostly broad and narrowing toward the tip. Some have scalloped edges, some indented, and some smooth. The leaves are normally densely covered in short hair, which resembles velvet. They are often shades of fawn to dark brown, usually lighter on the underside of the leaf. One form of it completely lacks this hair and has shiny green leaves. Another popular form, grown as a houseplant, has warts on the underside of its leaves, making it look like melted wax.

This plant has large, velvety leaves.

These large-growing plants from Madagascar have sturdy, woody trunks and a lax terminal rosette of leaves. They are susceptible to low temperatures. Plants can be propagated from the leaves. A leaf cut from the main stem, allowed to dry for a few days, and then planted will make a cluster of new plants from the base. Alternatively, sever the veins in the leaf in several places and hang it on a wire and, in time, the leaves will produce new plantlets from around each cut. These can be detached, rooted down, and grown on. Not all the offsets will be identical in color. Grow at a minimum temperature of 50°F (10°C), in a full-depth pot, and repot regularly as the plants grow, perhaps several times a year for optimum growth. Grow them in full sun or light shade.

Kalanchoe daigremontianum (syn. Bryophyllum daigremontianum)

This common houseplant grows to about 2–3 feet (60–100cm) tall and has long, boat-shaped leaves that are dark green to pink-green that are in some plants broad, in others narrow, or broad near the base and narrowing to the tip. The edge of the leaves is indented and from each indent a bulbil will grow.

This plant reproduces by producing new plantlets along the edge of the leaves.

The bulbils are small, new plants and are very easily detached. They will grow almost anywhere, in a carpet, on curtains, or wherever they drop. This tends to make it a very prolific plant, in other words, a weed.

There are several other Bryophyllum, all with the same characteristics. These are interesting succulent plants to grow and many children find them fascinating and very easy to propagate. They tend to be biennials but there is never any need to specifically propagate it. Just throw away untidy or dying plants.

Kalanchoe farinaceae

This species appears from time to time as a potted plant.

This interesting species from the isle of Socotra appears occasionally in horticulture as a potted plant. It is not a very easy plant to grow and needs a minimum temperature of 50°F (10°C) in winter. It will grow to about 1 foot (30cm) tall with a cluster of roundish leaves near stem tips. Its tubular flowers are reddish in color.

This plant only seems to branch sparingly, unless its stem tip is removed or damaged. It soon grows top-heavy and is best started each year from a cutting. While the white farina-covered leaves are very attractive, it is probably not a plant for the newer collector.

Kalanchoe hildebrandtii

This bushy Madagascan species is easy to grow, providing 50°F (10°C) can be maintained in winter. It can grow quite large, 10 feet (3m) or more in height, and has gray, felt-like leaves. In spring each branch produces spikes of small, creamy yellow flowers.

This species makes an attractive plant when about 1 foot (30cm) tall or larger. It is a leafy succulent and would fit well with other groups of plants. It is ideal for conservatories and easy to grow. Keep it well-watered in summer and prune from time to time to maintain a good shape.

These bushy plants flower easily in spring.

Kalanchoe pumila

This small-growing species is an ideal plant for a hanging basket. It has trailing stems and small, mealy white leaves. The small pink flowers are produced in the spring.

This is not a difficult plant to grow and prefers a bright situation but not full sun. It seems to want more water than many succulents during the summer. The long stems can be very brittle, but any bits that break off can be easily rooted to make new plants.

These plants make ideal hanging basket specimens.

If grown in a hanging basket, any long and straggly bits should be cut back in the spring to encourage the plant to branch from near the base and make a denser plant. A minimum temperature of 50°F (10°C) in winter is recommended.

Kalanchoe tomentosa

This bushy species from Madagascar will grow to 2–3 feet (60–100cm) tall, but is usually seen as much smaller plants in cultivation. Its stems are woody and branching, and its leaves are fleshy ovate in shape and densely covered in short hair, making them appear velvety. These leaves are normally pale colored with darker hairs near their tips. These can be shades of brown to dark brown and reddish. Each plant has its own unique color.

The velvety leaves have various colored markings at their tip.

This is quite a popular plant in cultivation and has been given the common name of panda plant. It is popular with children, as it has such soft, furry leaves. This species seems to grow best with partial shade and more frequent watering in summer. It is not a slow-growing plant and should be pruned from time to time to keep a good shape. Ever so often this plant will need to be started again from cuttings, as it becomes very woody and its foliage is sparse.

Kalanchoe 'Wendy'

This horticultural hybrid is a popular hanging basket plant that flowers in the spring. It is easy to grow and flower, but prefers shade to full sun. After flowering, cut the plant back to remove the old flowering stems and tidy the plant. Later in the year, about August, prune it again to shorten any long and out of place stems. The plant will then branch out and start to grow before it starts to initiate its buds in the autumn months.

Most Kalanchoes flower after a period of short days, which naturally means they flower in the spring. As most respond quite easily to adjustments in day length, this is a popular plant in the horticultural trade, as it can be made to flower at any time of year. If successive batches of plants are worked on, it is possible to buy one in flower throughout the year.

This is popular as a hanging basket plant.

Lampranthus haworthii

The Lampranthus are shrubby Mesembryanthemums that produce daisy-like flowers, usually in bright colors. In frost-free areas, these are used extensively as bedding plants.

Most Lampranthus are too large-growing for the windowsill or small glasshouse, but can be used as summer bedding plants, or feature plants in pots in areas that are not frost-free.

Lampranthus haworthii is a beautiful subject for flowers in spring.

Lampranthus haworthii is eventually a large-growing bush, which has spectacular bright pink flowers in the spring. The 2 inch (5cm) diameter flowers are produced in such profusion that they completely cover the plant. The flowers are also lightly perfumed. It is a species that will tolerate low temperatures in winter, but not coupled with high humidity, and can be grown outdoors in areas that seldom receive frosts. After flowering, the plants, should be pruned back to shape, keeping in mind that it will be considerably larger by the next flowering season.

This species flowers when quite small and even as a small plant is attractive, with its long, round, blue-green leaves and spring flowers.

Lampranthus roseus

This spreading species is rapid-growing and is a good groundcover plant in frost-free areas. It flowers with its pale pink flowers on and off throughout the spring and summer. Prune it back from time to time to keep it under control.

Like many of the shrubby Mesembryanthums, this plant will become woody at the base, which will limit its life span. It is a good idea to start new plants from time to time and replace old plants.

An easy plant to grow, it is suitable for summer bedding or landscape planting.

This succulent flowers during summer.

Lithops aucampiae, L. optica, L. pseudotruncatella

Lithops pseudotruncatella is one of the first Lithops to flower each year.

Lithops are a group of about 50 species of highly succulent Mesembryanthums. The plant is composed of two swollen leaves, united for most of their length, and shaped at the top, or like an inverted cone. The common name for these plants is stone plants or living stones.

The plants from above are roughly oval in shape, with a fissure between the two leaves. In some species, the flat-topped leaves are slightly different sizes, making them appear slightly kidney shaped. The flowers are produced in the autumn and are either white or yellow, depending on species, and open fully in sunshine, usually in the afternoons.

The plants in this genus are fairly similar. Their differences are the size of the fissure between the leaves, the type of markings on them, the flower color, and other minor points. The color of the plants varies between new and old leaves and a range is usual for most species. These plants are some of the most sensitive to over watering, although they will tolerate near freezing temperatures if

Lithops aucampiae is a very variable large headed species.

completely dry. It is important to understand their growing season in order to grow them well. Their autumn flowering is really the end of their growing season and they should then be kept dry until the following spring. During this time, their old leaves will usually shrivel, transferring their nutrients to a new pair of leaves that emerge at right angles from the fissure between the old leaves. In the spring, these plants should be watered from time to time, until early summer. The plants then grow until the autumn when those old enough will flower again. As the flowers are terminal, those that have flowered will normally make two pairs of leaves the following year.

Lithops optica is one of the few green Lithops.

Lithops are easy to grow from seed but need slightly different growing conditions until they are mature and reach flowering size. Seedlings are not quite so prone to rotting and need a little more water than mature plants. They will change their skins several times during the year as these plants grow. They should be treated much the same as cacti are. Use a very well-drained compost to avoid water logging the compost. Mix one volume of cactus compost with an equal volume of fine grit for good results. Seedlings should be grown in a very bright situation, but perhaps not in full sun in lower latitudes.

Nananthus vittatus

These are small, tuberous, rooted plants that clump freely to make very short stems with about four leaves per head. The leaves are dark olive green to brownish green and thickened with a flat to slightly concave upper surface and a keeled lower one. The plants flower during the autumn–spring period when weather conditions are warm enough and there is some bright sunlight. The flowers are about ½ inch (1cm) across, shades of yellow with a red central stripe on each petal.

Nananthus vittatus flowers easily from autumn to spring.

These are easy plants to grow from seed but need well-drained compost. As the plants are tuberous, they are more prone to rotting in wet compost than many fibrous, rooted plants. Their main growing season is from autumn to spring, with a semi dormant period in the heat of summer. Old plants with a large tuber are more temperamental and need more careful watering than seedlings.

An attractive dwarf, leafy Mesembryanthum, it reliably flowers from about a year old at a time of year when there is little else out in flower. It is well worth growing, even on a windowsill.

Neohenrichia sibbettii

This is a very small-growing, carpeting Mesembryanthum. It has very small leaves that are club-shaped and covered in raised warts. The flowers are very small, normally white, and often very sweetly scented. This is a very attractive small carpeting species that is easy to grow. It seems to want more water than many other species and can be prone to desiccating in long periods of drought.

This small-headed carpeting species prefers damper conditions than many species.

It is an easy plant to propagate by small cuttings that seem to root quite easily. Grow it in well-drained compost in a shallow pan. Its leaves are very similar (but much smaller) than a Titanopsis. This is well worth growing in any collection.

Pachyphytum oviferum

The sugared almond plant is closely related to the Echeverias. It has almond-shaped leaves in a rosette at the tips of its stems, which are covered in a powdery farina. This is easily removed by contact with the leaves, which are very lightly attached to the stems, making them very easy to accidentally knock off. The flowers are produced on short, arched flower stems, much the same color as the leaves. From below, you can see the red insides to each flower. This makes it an ideal plant to grow in a hanging basket.

The common name for this species is the sugared almond plant.

This plant branches freely from the base and soon makes fine clumps. Plants grown in a bright situation, but out of full sun, and given enough water, will grow much more quickly and make much fuller plants than those grown in full sun, but will not be quite so densely covered in farina.

These plants are easy to propagate from cuttings. Rerooting the terminal rosettes can propagate old plants that have become untidy, or have very long stems. An easy way to make more plants is to remove some of the lower leaves and allow them to dry for a few days, and then to set them into very gritty compost. These will soon root down and after 3–6 months will have developed several new plants from the buried end of each leaf. This is an attractive plant to grow on a windowsill or as a houseplant, apart from a glasshouse.

Pleiospilos compactus

Sometimes called living granite, this Mesembryanthums has a few thick swollen gray-brown-green leaves that are covered in darker dots. In the past, there have been many plants in this genus that were almost impossible to separate. These have now been reduced to four species. Three species are very distinct with

This plant is commonly known as living granite.

large swollen leaves, usually two per plant or per stems, but these species seldom branch. The rest are now included in *P. compactus*.

These plants usually branch quite freely and have thick, fleshy leaves that are narrowed toward the tip with a flattish upper surface. The leaves are thick and keeled. Usually plants will have between 4–8 leaves per stem, depending how much water is given to them. Plants will in time become quite well branched, the branches usually spreading sideways. This entire genus has large bright yellow flowers mostly in autumn, which are often coconut scented. These bright flowers are attractive at a time of year when there are not many flowers on cacti.

These are easy plants to grow from seed and flower at about 2 years old. Plants seem tolerant of low temperatures if dry. The main growth is from late spring until late autumn, so be sparing with water in the early part of the year or plants are liable to rot.

Portulacaria afra

Sometimes called a penny plant because of its small roundish leaves, this is a shrubby plant with many branches, and growing to about 12 feet (4m) tall. Its stems are reddish brown in color and branch freely. The side branches are mostly slender and the weight of the leaves gives the plant a "weeping" habit. In frost-free areas it is sometimes used as a hedging plant, as it can be quite quick growing when supplied with sufficient water.

It also makes an attractive houseplant and needs regular pruning to keep a good shape. This is an easy plant to

This plant makes an attractive house plant but needs regular pruning.

root from cuttings. Grow it in a reasonably sized pot in full sun and feed it well during the growing season. Any size of plant is attractive. There is also a variegated form with yellow, green, and red-marked leaves. This is much slower growing, but is attractive even on a windowsill.

Sedum morganianum and S. burrito

The Sedums are naturally widespread throughout the world. Many are completely hardy and usually classed with Alpines or rockery plants. It is usually only those from more temperate areas that are cultivated by cacti collectors.

Sedum morganianum is a pedant species with short, pale green-blue leaves that are pointed at both ends. They are densely arranged in spirals around the stem, pointing toward the stem tip. They are very lightly attached to the stem making it a difficult plant to move or repot without dislodging at least some of

Sedum burrito has shorter fatter leaves.

them. This species
makes a very attractive
houseplant and prefers
light shade to full sun.
Grown well in a hanging
basket, the stems can
hang to nearly 6 feet
(2m) in length. In the
spring, many of the
longer stems will pro-
duce their clusters of
small, red flowers at the
end of the stem. After
flowering, the stems
usually branch. From
time to time, old stems
that have become bald
of leaves should be
removed to allow new
stems to develop.
These plants seem
capable of growing
throughout the year
when conditions are

Sedum morganianum flowers in spring.

suitable. Keep them dry in winter at lower temperatures.

Sedum burrito is very similar and was for some while thought to be a hybrid,
but is now considered a species in its own right. Its leaves are shorter, slightly
fatter, and denser on the stems.

Sedum rubrotinctum

This short, bushy species forms large colonies. Its cylindrical leaves are rounded at their tips and a dark glossy green in color. Grown in full sun, they become bright red in color. This is a very easy plant to grow and is well distributed as a houseplant. Plants propagate themselves from fallen leaves, which rapidly root and make new plants. Clusters of yellow flowers are produced during the spring–summer period.

In the shade these plants are dark green, in full sun they turn bright red.

There is also an attractive cultivar 'Aurora' which has bright pink and green leaves. It is slightly more compact than the species and is easily propagated from stem cuttings. Often rooted leaves revert back to the green form. In order to preserve its attractive color, remove any stems that have reverted to green or they will outgrow the cultivar.

Senecio articulatus

Commonly known as the candle plant, this species has blue-green stems and a terminal rosette of bluish, triangular, succulent leaves on longish stalks. Below the leaf bases, usually the stems have markings that look like a bird's foot. This is a remarkably robust species and able to tolerate complete neglect for a long period, but will not tolerate gross over watering. It is a plant that is normally dormant through the height of summer.

This plant is quite common in cultivation and its growth pattern directly relates to the amount of food and water it gets in the growing season. If it is grown in rich compost and kept well watered during the growing season, then it is possible for its stems to grow about 4 feet (1.2m) long. If on the other hand it is grown in very gritty, open and free draining compost with a minimum amount of water, the stems will be no more than an inch (2.5cm) in length and like little barrels. This makes a far more beautiful plant, as the long straggly stems are very brittle and liable to break off the plant under their weight. Probably a compromise between the two is best, but erring on the "poorly grown" end of the scale.

The candle plant grows throughout the winter.

The plants produce their heads of tiny ¼ inch (0.5cm) diameter flowers in the autumn that can have a rather noxious odor and are perhaps better removed.

Senecio haworthii

This is probably the whitest of all the Senecios. It is a bush up to about 2 feet (60cm) tall, which spreads to make large clumps. Its leaves are almost cylindrical, pointed toward the tip and completely covered in brilliant white felt. The leaves

are produced in lax rosettes at the tops of the stem, which gradually become long and straggly with just a few leaves at the tip. These old stems are best removed and can also be used to make fresh cuttings for propagation. A well grown plant is beautiful but it does need regular pruning to cut out the old and allow the new to grow.

Prune out old long stems to keep an attractive plant.

This makes a beautiful potted plant but in frost-free areas, it is spectacular as a bedding plant, making a wonderful splash of white in the garden. It is an easy plant to grow and propagate.

Senecio kleinia

This bushy or tree-like species grows to about 10 feet (3m) tall. It has terminal rosettes of long spear shaped leaves, which are broader in some forms than others. Its succulent stems become quite woody with age, but the young growth can be quite brittle. The plants are summer dormant, flowering in late summer with terminal spikes of groundsel like flowers. Soon after this, the plants will come into leaf and grow through until mid spring when they will stop growing. Then the leaves will slowly wither to leave almost bare sticks in summer.

This is an easy plant to grow from seed, or from non-woody cuttings. These however need to be taken in the summer and rooted in early autumn, as they too will go dormant in spring. Young plants look a little like a miniature palm tree, which makes them popular as houseplants.

These tall, bushy plants produce leaflets in summer.

Senecio rowleyanus

A popular houseplant, and often known as string of beads, is *Senecio rowleyanus*. It has very slender, creeping stems and produces round, very swollen, succulent leaves, like small peas. It naturally creeps along the ground, branching and rebranching, rooting as it goes, to make dense mats. In cultivation, it is much better grown in a hanging basket, so that the trailing stems can hang down to produce a "bead curtain." The tiny groundsel-like flowers are very sweetly scented.

It is an easy plant to grow and does not really like long periods of drought, although it will survive them. It likes a moderate amount of water, but the roots can rot if kept permanently wet.

It is an easy plant to propagate from cuttings in the spring to autumn. Either lay the stems across a tray of compost and let them root down naturally, or divide the pieces of stem into sections about 3–4 inches (7.5–10cm) long and lay them on the surface of small individual pots. Keep them damp and they will grow quite quickly.

The string of beads makes a good hanging basket plant.

Senecio serpens

This attractive carpeting species with powdery blue leaves and creeping stems is often used in frost-free areas as a ground cover plant. This plant has long, semi-cylindrical leaves and makes stems that grow 4–5 inches (10–12cm) tall, after which they become prostate and trailing. The plant also produces underground stems, all of which will regularly root down to make quite large colonies. This plant is quite popular as a potted plant with its powdery blue leaves. As such, it

The powdery blue leaves make this an attractive groundcover plant.

needs regular pruning to remove long and straggly stems and allow the fresh new stems to develop.

It is an easy plant to grow and propagate. It likes a reasonable amount of water, but not wet conditions. When it is dry, its leaves become concave on their upper surface and limp.

Trichodiadema bulbosum

This fascinating genus of Mesembryanthums have at the end of each leaf a cluster of small hairs, much like an areole and cluster of fine spines. These plants can be very compact, trailing, or bushy with a wide range of flower colors. They

are all interesting plants to grow and most flower quite freely throughout the summer.

Trichodiadema bulbosum is a smaller growing species that is sometimes cultivated as a bonsai. As the plants grow, they make an underground storage tuber that in time will grow above the ground. From this it produces one to three stems that are thick at the base, and as they grow, make numerous side branches. In the wild these are fairly short but in cultivation they can grow to more than 6 inches (14cm) long. Each small cylindrical leaf is covered in bright papillae, which make them glisten in

These plants make a large underground tuber which can be raised and potted like a bush.

the sun. At the end of each leaf is a small diadem of pale brown "spines" that will gradually darken to brown as the plant ages. These plants produce numerous small, bright, dark pink flowers during the summer–autumn period.

People who want to cultivate this plant as a bonsai wait until it has developed a reasonably sized tuber and then lift it in the pot until about half of it is exposed. The top growth is mostly cut away, leaving just a short main stem. It is then grown with little water and will slowly develop short stems.

To grow in a more conventional manner, use well-drained compost and avoid overwatering. Keep it dry in winter.

Trichodiadema densum

This is a small, compact, clump-forming plant. It has very short internodes and its small cylindrical leaves are covered in papillae. Its diadems at the ends of its leaves have numerous longish white bristles that partially obscure the plant.

Bright red-purple flowers are produced from time to time during the summer months.

This very compact plant is perhaps the prettiest in this genus. It is not difficult to grow, but needs well-drained compost and will rot in wet conditions. Allow to dry between waterings and keep dry in winter. Propagate from seeds or cuttings.

Small dense bushes produce bright flowers in summer.

Index